BRITISH MOTORCYCLE
RACING CIRCUITS
Since 1907

England, Scotland, Wales, Isle of Man and Northern Ireland

BRITISH MOTORCYCLE
RACING CIRCUITS
Since 1907

England, Scotland, Wales, Isle of Man and Northern Ireland

MICK WALKER

breedon **books**
PUBLISHING

First published in Great Britain in 2008 by
The Breedon Books Publishing Company Limited
Breedon House, 3 The Parker Centre,
Derby, DE21 4SZ.

Dedication

With grateful thanks to my friend and fellow enthusiast Elwyn Roberts, who
kindly provided many of the programmes used in the making of this book,
and much encouragement for the project.

ISBN 978-1-85983-657-6
UPC 8 262051 0015 0

Printed and bound by Scotprint, Haddington, Scotland

CONTENTS

PREFACE 9

HOW IT ALL BEGAN 11

SOUTH EAST 14
Alexandra Palace 14
Biggin Hill 15
Boreham 15
Brands Hatch 18
Brooklands 22
Crystal Palace 26
Goodwood 29
Grandsden Lodge 30
Long Marston 31
Lydden Hill 31
North Weald 32
Paddington 33
Sculthorpe 33
Snetterton 33
Stapleford Tawney 35
Thorney Island 36
Waterbeach 36
Welwyn Garden City 37
West Raynham 37

SOUTH WEST 38
Blandford 38
Bryanston Park 40
Castle Combe 41
Chivenor 44
Colerne 45
Goram Fair 45
Ibsley 46
Imber Road 47
Keevil 48

Little Rissington 48
Moreton Valence 50
Pendennis Castle 51
Plymouth 51
St Eval 51
Staverton 52
Sutton Veney 52
Thruxton 53
Weston-super-Mare 56
Wroughton 57
Wymering Park 57

MIDLANDS 58
Alton Towers 58
Ansty 60
Chirk Castle 62
Church Lawford 62
Darley Moor 62
Donington Park 63
Gamston 68
Gaydon 68
Haddenham 69
Hanley Park 70
Long Marston 70
Mallory Park 71
Osmaston Manor 75
Park Hall 76
Perton 78
Prees Heath 78
Retford Project 78
Rockingham 79
Rockingham Castle 79
Silverstone 80
Syston 84
Wellesbourne 84

NORTH EAST	85
Barkston Heath	85
Beadnell	86
Brough	86
Cadwell Park	89
Carnaby Raceway	93
Carnaby Two	95
Catterick Airfield	95
Catterick Camp	96
Croft	97
Elvington	98
Esholt	99
Everthorpe Park	101
Langbaurgh	101
Ormesby Hall	101
Ouston	102
Rufforth	102
Scarborough	102
Teesside Autodrome	106
Thornaby	107
Tranwell	107
West Park	107

NORTH WEST	108
Aintree	108
Altcar	110
Belle Vue	111
Flookburgh	111
Greeves Hall Project	112
Longridge	112
New Brighton	112
Oulton Park	113
Parbold	116
Silloth	117
Three Sisters	119

SCOTLAND	121
Alford	121
Ballado	121
Beveridge Park	122
Charterhall	124
Crail	124
Crimond	125
East Fortune	126
Edzell	129
Errol	130
Gask	132
Ingliston	133
Kennell	133
Knockhill	134
Turnbury	136
Winfield	136

WALES	137
Aberdare Park	137
Anglesey	140
Eppynt	140
Fairwood	143
Kinmel Park	143
Llandow	144
Mona	145
Pembrey	146
Rhydymwyn	147
St Athan	147
Tonfanau	148
Ty Croes	149

ISLE OF MAN	150
Andreas	150
Jurby	150
Manx Grand Prix	151
Southern 100	153
Tourist Trophy	156

NORTHERN IRELAND 166

Aghadowey	167
Aldergrove Airfield	168
Ballydrain	168
Ballykelly Airfield	168
Ballynahinch	168
Banbridge – Bann 50	168
Banbridge 100	169
Bangor Castle	169
Bishopcourt	169
Bush – Dungannon Revival Meeting	169
Carrowdore 100	170
Clandeboye	171
Coleraine 100	171
Comber	171
Cookstown 100	172
Desertmartin	173
Dundrod 100	173
Dundrod 150	173
Dundrod 200	173
Dungannon 100	174
Enniskillen 100	174
Greengraves	175
Killinchy 150	175
Killough	175
Kirkistown	175
Lisburn 100	177
Long Kesh Airfield	177
Lurgan Park	177
Maghaberry	177
Mid-Antrim 100	178
Mid-Antrim 150	179
Monaghan – Glaslough Circuit	180
Newtownards Airport	180
North Down 60	180
North West 200	180
Nutts Corner	183
St Angelo	183
Tandragee 100	183
Temple 100	183
Ulster Grand Prix	185
Ulster 100	189

APPENDIX 190

Circuit/Events in Southern Ireland (Eire)	190

INDEX 192

Every so often a unique snapshot of times gone by is discovered in a dusty vault or in shoeboxes in an attic by an enthusiastic amateur photographer. They are living history. Each and every one of us cannot resist the temptation as we marvel at the quality of the images, to let our mind drift back to the good old days and wonder what it was really like.

We at Mortons Motorcycle Media, market-leading publishers of classic and vintage titles, own one of the largest photographic archives of its kind in the world. It is a treasure trove of millions of motorcycle and related images, many of which have never seen the light of day since they were filed away in the dark-room almost 100 years ago.

Perhaps the biggest gem of all is our collection of glass plates – almost two tons of them to be precise! They represent a largely hitherto unseen look into our motorcycling heritage from the turn of the century. Many of the plates are priceless and capture an era long gone when the pace of life was much slower and traffic jams were unheard of.

We are delighted to be associated with well known author Mick Walker in the production of this book and hope you enjoy the images from our archive.

Terry Clark,
Managing Director,
Mortons Media Group Ltd

PREFACE

British Motorcycle Racing Circuits Since 1907 has turned out to be one of the most interesting among the 110-odd books that I have been fortunate enough to write over the last quarter of a century. Why? Well, the more I got into the project the more enthusiastic I became. Besides the famous venues such as Brands Hatch, Silverstone, Mallory Park, Snetterton and Oulton Park came my own favourites, Cadwell Park, Scarborough and, perhaps obviously, the Isle of Man Mountain course.

But, of course, these few were to prove very much the tip of the iceberg. Some, such as Bryanston Park, Bangor Castle, Goram Fair, Gransden Lodge and Rockingham Castle, only held a single meeting many years ago. Then there was Brooklands with all its history. The likes of Alexandra Palace and Alton Towers may not be familiar names as racing circuits, but they most certainly are for other reasons.

Scotland, Wales and Northern Ireland all had numerous circuits, many of which are only familiar to the country concerned but are still vital to the completeness of this book.

There were many, many circuits thanks to the use of military bases – not just former or existing airfields, but other Ministry of Defence establishments. Another significant source of venues were the many estates and parks, some of which survive to the present day, but the vast majority long since forgotten with the passage of time.

In pre-war days several circuits were little more than paths, while the birth of 50cc racing even saw the use of existing cycle tracks, repeating a tradition that had been used at the very turn of the 20th century with the likes of White City, Canning Town and Herne Hill.

I must confess that prior to beginning the project several of the names were unfamiliar to me – remember this book goes back over 100 years! The fact is, almost anywhere in Great Britain there was a race circuit somewhere very near to where you live now.

Then there were the host of old friends and new friends who kindly helped me with information, photographs, or even personal memories. In particular I salute the following, in no particular order of merit: Bill and Agnes Cadger, Hugh Ward, David Pike, Vic Bates, Wolfgang Gruber, the late Bill Lomas, Peter Reeve, Brenda Scivyer, Ian and Rita Welsh, Ken Turner, Phil Morris, Richard Agnew, Harry Havland, George and Archie Plenderleith, Nigel Clark, John Patrick, Dougie and Susan Muir, Reg Everett, Dave Edwards (Aintree Motorcycle Racing Club), Rodney Gooch (Castle Combe), John Mottram, Peter Hillaby and the Auto 66 Club, Steve Bedford, Bill Snelling, Mike Ward (Grampian Transport Museum), Margaret King, Martyn Perry, Fred Pidcock and Elwyn Roberts.

I just hope you, the reader, gain as much enjoyment from reading *British Motorcycle Racing Circuits Since 1907* as I have had compiling it.

Mick Walker,
Wisbech, Cambridgeshire

HOW IT ALL BEGAN

The 20th century was just six years old, Edward VII benevolently ruled a widespread empire in a world at peace – kept that way largely by dreadnoughts and gunboats, Sam Brownes and Short Lee Enfields. Hansom cabs still clip-clopped around in the capital, but in the mews of Belgravia and Kensington coachmen were rapidly becoming chauffeurs. Henry Royce was building 'the world's best motor cars' and his partner, the Hon. Charles Rolls, was racing them and selling them to the nobility and gentry.

Motor-Bicyclists

In a somewhat lower social stratum an ever-increasing band of enthusiastic motor-bicyclists had firmly established themselves as a fraternity as well organised as the sporting motorists. Founded on the lines of the Automobile Club of Great Britain and Northern Ireland (later to become the RAC – Royal Automobile Club), the Auto Cycle Club was their governing body, and it was at the 1906 annual dinner of the club that the idea of a motorcycle Tourist Trophy race was first propounded.

It came from one of the after-dinner speakers, H.W. Stainer, magazine editor of *The Motor Cycle*. While proposing the toast of 'the Sport and Pastime' he mentioned the Tourist Trophy races for cars, which were being held in the Isle of Man. Why, he asked, could there not be a similar event for motorcycles? He suggested limits on engine displacement and machine weight, with the objective of demonstrating the reliability and efficiency of roadgoing motorcycles.

The ACC committee took up the idea but decided that a better way of exploiting the touring aspect would be to place the emphasis on fuel consumption so as to demonstrate and develop not only the reliability of motorcycles, but also their economy.

The Isle of Man

The choice of the Isle of Man was a logical one. With a 20mph (31.1km/h) speed limit enforced in the United Kingdom, the only practical venues for speed events on public roads were the continent and Ireland. The Isle of Man, with its own parliament, could not only close its roads but its authorities were by then accustomed to collaborating in the organisation and welcomed 'racers'. Furthermore, the ACC folk were no strangers to

Manxland, having the previous year held speed selection trials over Manx roads in preparation for the International Cup Race in Europe.

On being approached the island government readily gave its consent to a motorcycle TT and the ACC set about organising it.

The Marquis

Except that the motorcycling press of the day almost invariably described him as 'the well-known sportsman', not much is known about the Marquis de Mouzilly St Mars. How he – presumably a Frenchman – came to link up with the TT project is not clear, but we all know the practical outcome, for it took the form of the Tourist Trophy itself.

Given by the Marquis for the best performance in the single-cylinder class of the race, this handsome, valuable, 2ft 10in (86.3cm) high silver figure of Mercury poised on a winged-wheel later became the Senior Trophy. In its 100-plus years it has been repaired many times, and in 1939 it disappeared into Germany, turning up in Italy in 1945, where it was found by Australian TT rider, Arthur Simcock.

For the twin-cylinder class a silver rose bowl was presented by another sportsman, Doctor Hele-Shaw, who was a member of the ACC committee. This award, however, disappeared permanently very early in TT history.

At the beginning of the 20th century cycle tracks at venues such as White City and Canning Town were used before purpose-built circuits came into use.

To select a suitable course, a party of club officials, led by the secretary, F. Straight, visited the island early in 1907. The car racers were then using a circuit that began in Douglas, went direct to Peel, then to Kirkmichael and Ramsey and back over Snaefell Mountain; however, this was judged too steep for motorcycles at that time, and instead a triangular 15.8-mile (25.4km) circuit was chosen. The details of this are fully described in chapter 9. The first TT took place on Tuesday 28 May 1907, and so specialised British motorcycle circuit racing began.

Beside the Isle of Man, the other notable early venue for the sport was conceived in 1906 by wealthy landowner Hugh Locke-King and his wife Dame Ethal. The Brooklands track on a 30-acre section of his estate, near Weybridge, Surrey, opened for car racing in July the following year with motorcycles following in spring 1908. The design work for this is credited to Royal Engineers Colonel Capel Holden and took a work force of some 2,000 nine months to complete. The 2.75-mile (4.42km) steeply banked track cost £150,000 (many millions in today's money!) and came from the Locke-King coffers.

As mentioned above, the first motorcycle racing activity at Brooklands was not until 1908, when two machines raced over a single lap during a Brooklands Automobile Racing Club car meeting. The winner, W.G. McMinnies on a 3.5hp single-cylinder Triumph, averaged 58.8mph (94.6km/h) over the flying half mile. The first true open motorcycle race was held at the Surrey circuit on Easter Monday of the same year.

And so began motorcycle circuit racing in Great Britain and, as this book reveals, these venues have been far more numerous than anyone in those pioneering days could ever have imagined. *British Motorcycle Racing Circuits* is that story; enjoy!

SOUTH EAST

Alexandra Palace (1935)
Biggin Hill (1959)
Boreham (1950–52)
Brands Hatch (1950–)
Brooklands (1908–39)
Crystal Palace (1927–72)
Goodwood (1951 and 1998–)
Gransden Lodge (1946)
Long Marston (1970s)
Lydden Hill (1965–)
North Weald (1946)
Paddington (1962)
Sculthorpe (early 1990s)
Snetterton (1953–)
Stapleford Tawney (1947)
Thorney Island (1977)
Waterbeach (mid-1970s)
Welwyn Garden City (1962)
West Raynham (late 1970s)

Note:
Years quoted above relate to use as motorcycle road race circuits and not other uses (i.e. other branches of two-wheel sport, or cars). This format is repeated throughout the other chapters.

ALEXANDRA PALACE

In 1935 London could claim to have a northern circuit in addition to the already existing Crystal Palace south of the Thames. For many months before, the North East London MCC had been negotiating for the use of a circuit at the Alexandra Palace. The course was roughly triangular in shape, with two of the sides more than twice the length of the third. For the greater part the surface was of tarmac, but there was one long stretch of gravel. The circuit measured one and a half miles (2.14km) and ran anti-clockwise.

The first meeting was staged on Saturday 27 July 1935 and included names such as Tommy Wood, Tom Arter and Jack Surtees (the latter in the sidecar race).

A second meeting took place on Saturday 24 August and, as before, the circuit was more suitable for the 350 rather than the 500ccs in the solo races. It also included a 10-lap Unlimited solo event for the North East London Cup which featured a 'Le Mans' start, where competitors lined up opposite their machines and then sprinted across the road to leap aboard at the drop of the flag.

Unlike Crystal Palace, road racing at Alexandra Palace was not continued, probably because the circuit was pretty dangerous due to a combination of various surfaces and widths, a steep hilly section with an equally steep incline elsewhere, and even tram lines; the latter, in the wet, being lethal!

Biggin Hill

Biggin Hill, between New Addington and Sevenoaks, Kent, gained fame as a fighter base for the RAF during the Battle of Britain. It also hosted a trio of road race meetings in 1959 on 21 June, 9 August and 4 October, over a one-mile (1.61km) airfield circuit, organised by The Double Five Kent Motor Club.

At the first meeting Ginger Payne was the star, winning the 350 and 1000cc races on Nortons and bringing the REG twin home second behind Dan Shorey's Norvel in the 250cc event. At the August meeting it was Phil Read's turn in the 350cc event, with Shorey a double winner (125 and 250cc), while Alan Trow and Ed Minihan shared a victory each in the 1000cc races. At the third meeting riders such as Mike Hailwood and Derek Minter showed up, with the former emerging victorious in the 200, 250, 350 and 1000cc races.

Controversy raged the following spring when in March 1960 news came through that opposition from local residents had stopped the organising club's April fixture at Biggin Hill. Apparently the local Orpington Council, after receiving a petition from local residents, had asked the Air Ministry to ban future road racing at the venue; however, the club had been unable to find out exactly how many people signed the petition – or, indeed, whether a petition had actually even been lodged! That signalled the end for the circuit.

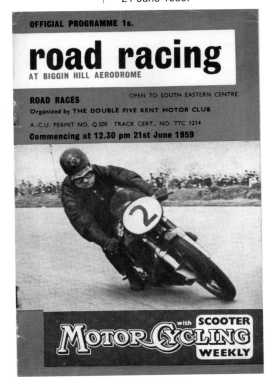

Biggin Hill programme from 21 June 1959.

Boreham

As *The Motor Cycle* reported, 'Riders and spectators alike expressed great satisfaction with the course the Chelmsford

Advertisements from 1951
(top) and 1952.

Boreham racing
circuit, 1952.

Club had laid out on Boreham Aerodrome for a road racing programme featuring the "Chelmsford 100" on September 2.' Motorcycle events at this Essex venue started in 1950.

As was to be expected, the '100' title of the big race was in respect of its 100-mile (160.9km) distance. And it was won by George Brown riding his 998cc Vincent HRD Black Lightning with a fastest lap of 87.5mph (140.8km/h).

At the time, many observers thought that the Boreham circuit could become a serious rival to Goodwood or Silverstone. The track, almost three miles (4.827km) long, was certainly wide enough and lent itself to high lap speeds.

At the start was a quarter-mile (0.4km) straight with a slight downhill slope, followed by a gentle left-hand bend which could be negotiated flat-out, followed by another straight section. A right-hand curve led into Waltham Corner, practically a 180-degree turn, and from there into Tower Bend. After this came a straight section, round Orchard Corner, and down into Duke's Straight. A 90-degree right-hander followed by a milder bend then led back to the finishing straight.

The first meeting of 1951, held at the end of April, saw George Brown very slightly improve on his existing lap record when winning the Unlimited race, from J.P.E. Hodgkin (both on 998cc Vincents), with a youthful John Surtees third on a 499cc Vincent Grey Flash. Other winners were Roland Pike (250cc), Robin Sherry (350cc) and Sid Barnett (500cc). The two sidecar races were won by Cyril Smith and Bill Boddice.

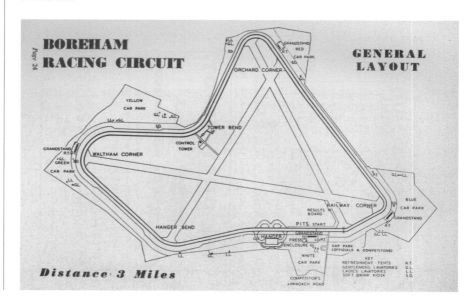

The next meeting in July saw Tony McAlpine (998cc Vincent HRD) set a new course lap record of 88.5mph (142.39km/h). This time Roland Pike was beaten in the 250cc by Cecil Sandford (Velocette), Robin Sherry won the 350cc and Ken Kavanagh the 500cc (and he was also runner-up in the 350cc), while no sidecar event was held. The final meeting of the year, held in early September, was spoiled by bad weather. Even so, the main race of the day, the Chelmsford 100, was won in pouring rain by John Surtees with his Vincent Grey Flash.

For the 1952 season, racing at Boreham was sponsored by the *Daily Mail* newspaper with dates of 26 April, 26 July, 3 August and 23 August. In the 20 March 1952 issue of *The Motor Cycle* it was reported that 'a racing organisation, to be called Motor Racing Co Ltd, has been formed to develop the Boreham, Essex airfield circuit. One of the major improvements to be made is the resurfacing of the three-mile [4.827km] track. It is hoped to make Boreham one of Europe's premier race circuits.'

Although Robin Sherry (348cc AJS) set a new lap record of 90.3mph (145.29km/h) at the April meeting, it was the state of the track that got most publicity. A typical press document of the time said, 'In many places the concrete runways had previously cracked and subsided. The work of resurfacing the entire circuit is now well under way, and it should be completely finished in time for the ACU International meeting.' Before this came the National meeting on 26 July, where not only had the resurfacing been completed, but a number of new riders were making their debuts at Boreham. Four large grandstands had been erected, together with a giant scoreboard in place (but not used on this occasion), and the public address system vastly improved.

The riders included Les Graham (MV Agusta), Ken Kavanagh (Nortons) and John Storr (also Norton mounted), plus circuit specialist Robin Sherry

Programme from 23 August 1952.

General view of Railway Corner during 500cc final, 1952. Les Graham (58, MV Agusta) is leading.

(works AJS). But it was the Australian, Kavanagh, who came out on top, winning both the 350 and 500cc races and setting a new course record of 95.24mph (153.24km/h). Besides the main two classes, there were also races for 125 and 250cc solos, plus sidecars.

Strangely, the ACU International Road Races were staged a week later over the Bank Holiday weekend; however, a combination of heavy rain, several high-profile non-arrivals (works FB Mondial and Montesa teams for example) and higher-than-expected spectator charges conspired to ensure that the crowd was considerably smaller than had been expected.

Again Ken Kavanagh was top man, with Les Graham (MV Agusta) winning the 125cc race and Fergus Anderson (Moto Guzzi) the 250cc class. Bill Boddice and Pip Harris were the top sidecar men.

At the end of August, Ken Kavanagh (348 and 499cc Nortons) won the bigger races for the third time running. In contrast to the rain-sodden 'International', the day was glorious for spectators and competitors alike – warm and dry with just enough cloud to prevent dazzle from the sun.

Nobody realised it at the time, but this was to be the last-ever motorcycle race meeting at Boreham. Since then the circuit has been used by the Ford Motor Company to test its competition cars in secrecy. As this book was being written, news came through that Ford has sold the site to property developers.

BRANDS HATCH

The origins of this famous circuit, situated on the Kentish Downs to the south east of London, dates back to 1926, when a group of passing cyclists noticed what they saw as a natural bowl – at that time a mushroom field – beside the road. This belonged to Brands Hatch farm. After discussion with the farmer, agreement was reached to allow the cyclists to compete there. Motorcycles arrived in 1928, but the first real signs of organisation came in 1932, when the Bermondsey, Owls, Sidcup and West Kent clubs joined forces to become the original Brands Hatch combines. Their first meeting – on the grass, as were all pre-war events – took place on 28 March.

Long before the Brands road racing era, the Kent venue was famous for its grass track events. Norton star Johnny Lockett is seen here with tuner Steve Lancefield in 1946.

The natural amphitheatre was ideal for spectators. The speeds grew and the oval grass track was extended to one mile (1.61km). After army occupation during World War Two, grass-tracking returned to Brands with some epic team battles between Brands and Wingfield (a grass circuit near Derby). In 1947 Brands Hatch Stadium Limited was created and a new Brands Racing Committee formed between the Gravesend Eagles, Rochester and Greenwich clubs.

During the closed season of 1949–50 the track was tarmaced, with the first race meeting being staged there on Easter Sunday, 9 April 1950. That first meeting in April 1950 saw several interesting names in the programme, including John Surtees (having his first-ever road race), his father Jack with passenger Charlie Rous (later to become a well-known journalist with *Motor Cycle News*), Alf Hagon, Bill Cheeson (later owner and founder of the Lydden Hill circuit), Vincent Davey (later boss of the London motorcycle dealership Gus Kuhn) and, perhaps most surprising of all, a certain Bernie Ecclestone (now the Formula One car supremo). By the end of that season, Jack Keel (riding Jock Hitchcock's Triumph 500 twin) held the lap record at 68.96mph (111km/h).

During the winter of 1951–52 the track was completely resurfaced. Soon afterwards, to overcome too many crashes going up Paddock Bend, an experiment was tried and one race staged the opposite way (clockwise, as now), and although speeds were slightly slower it was agreed that after 29 June 1952 all races would be run in a clockwise direction.

In 1953, Derek Minter made his debut at the Kent track aboard a BSA Gold Star. A year later and an extension loop was added between the end of Paddock Bend and the Bottom Straight, taking competitors up the 1:9 climb to Druids hairpin and down again to rejoin the old circuit at the Bottom Straight, bringing the lap distance up to 1.24 miles (2.00km). A crowd of over 45,000 watched the opening meeting on the longer course.

Newly erected grandstands were in place for spectators to witness the appearance of Geoff Duke and the Gilera four (his only Brands two-

Early programme from a grass track meeting, 6 April 1947.

Programme from the first race meeting on the new tarmaced track.

1952 advert for racing at Brands Hatch.

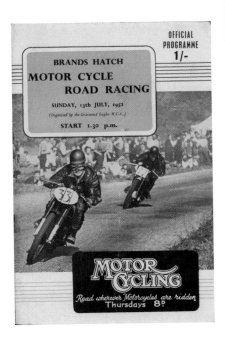

Brands Hatch programme, 13 July 1952.

The circuit plan from the 1955 programme, showing the new extended track up to Druids Hairpin.

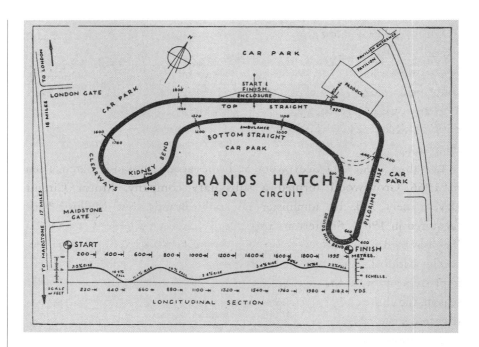

wheel appearance) in October 1955, but the multi-world champion had to settle for third behind local heroes John Surtees and Alan Trow (both Norton mounted). Then in 1957 both Alan Trow and Derek Minter separately beat Surtees, who was now riding the works four-cylinder MV Agusta. Minter continued his domination to earn the unofficial crown of 'King of Brands', with Bill Boddice doing the same in sidecar races.

Brands Hatch: the new 2.65-mile (4.26km) course, 1960. The first motorcycle meeting was on 9 July 1960.

On 9 July 1960 came the first meeting over the new 2.65-mile (4.26km) Grand Prix course. This extension utilised the old circuit and then turned left at South Bank Bend, going out into the winding and undulating countryside to rejoin the old circuit at Clearways. This initial meeting attracted over 40,000 fans and was the first full international permit meeting. Mike Hailwood won all four solo races after Minter crashed out of the proceedings.

Less than a year later Grovewood Securities acquired Brands Hatch. Then in 1966 Grovewood formed a subsidiary company, Motor Circuit Development Ltd, to administer not only Brands, but Mallory Park (acquired in 1962), Snetterton (1963) and Oulton Park (1964), with John Webb as managing director.

The paddock clubhouse, restaurant, startline control tower and other improvements were the next additions to the Kent circuit. After the 1974 season, the entire circuit was resurfaced, the first time it had been completely re-tarred since 1950.

To comply mainly with F1 car GP regulations, further work, including a new paddock, was completed in 1976. New infield pits forced a slightly different line at Bottom Straight, Paddock Bend was eased and the lap distance reduced to 2.61 miles (4.19km) and 1.2 miles (1.93km) for the short circuit (later called the Indy Circuit).

Further improvements have continued to be made, including the 'Kentagon' at the rear of Paddock Bend and later still, in the 1990s, the

1967 programme.

Plan of the circuit, showing the short course and the extended GP course.

1968 programme.

A view of Clearways and in the distance Paddock Hill Bend in the 1980s.

1981 programme.

Brands Hatch, 2 May 1983.
A jubilant Barry Sheene with
the new Transatlantic
Trophy, which depicted
maps of the three circuits
that year.

Foulston Centre (costing several millions) was completed after the Brands Hatch empire had been acquired by John Foulston. After John died in a car accident, his daughter Nicola was in charge for several years, before, finally, at the beginning of the 21st century, the Brands Hatch portfolio (now comprising Snetterton, Oulton Park and Cadwell Park) passed to Motor Sport Vision Ltd (with former F1 car racer Jonathan Palmer in the hot seat).

There is absolutely no doubt that Motor Sport Vision has made a significant improvement to all the circuits within its control, including, of course, Brands Hatch. And even more improvements are in the pipeline for the future.

During the 1970s Brands hosted the Transatlantic Challenge Series (with American and British teams battling it out annually). Many of the truly great names of the era contested these races, including Peter Williams, John Cooper, Cal Rayborn, Barry Sheene and Kenny Roberts. Another star of this period, the Italian Giacomo Agostini, won several top Brands races.

Next came the *Motor Cycle News* Superbike Championship. Then during the 1990s – and remaining today – Brands Hatch hosted the World Superbike Championships, together with the BSB (British Superbike) series. The WSB has often seen the crowds in excess of 100,000, making it the most popular of all mainland British motorcycle events.

As I am writing this, Brands Hatch is celebrating its 80th birthday. During that time it has risen from a purely local venue to one that is known around the world as a premier race circuit.

Brooklands

Brooklands, near Weybridge in Surrey, was not only Great Britain's first purpose-built racing circuit, but, until the outbreak of World War Two in September 1939, the hub of racing on the mainland. Like the Isle of Man TT, Brooklands opened in 1907, but the first motorcycle meeting was not staged until Easter Monday 1908.

Upon the official announcement that Brooklands was to be lost in 1946, *The Motor Cycle* in its 17 January issue that year painted a vivid picture for its readers of how this great circuit began:

'Let us go back to the opening years of the 20th century. Where Brooklands now lies there were green meadows and cowslips, quiet pine copses and banks of rhododendrons, and the blue, electric flash of kingfishers was commonly seen over the placid reaches of the river Wey. Then in 1906–07 the silence was rudely shattered. Gangs of navvies [some 2,000] and puffing steam-engines arrived at the quiet square-mile of the country, and the great concrete saucer gradually seared the virgin earth in a vast oval.'

A view of the Brooklands track and its banking, taken in August 1936.

Construction took some nine months, and the design is credited to Royal Engineers Colonel Capel Holden (maker of the Holden four-cylinder motorcycle). The cost of this venture was a reported £150,000, which in today's terms is many millions of pounds.

The circuit comprised the main Railway Straight, followed by the awesome Byfleet Banking, a shorter straight and then the tighter radius Home and Members Banking, the lap being conducted in an anti-clockwise direction.

From a spectator's point of view this was a very good layout, for the entire circuit could be seen from any one vantage point. So large was the complex that its infield contained an aerodrome complex with landing strip and hangers.

This purpose-built racing complex was probably the first significant civil engineering project in Britain to be constructed in concrete. Concrete technology was in its infancy in 1907, and the finished track surface was very bumpy, nothing like the smooth surface of today's motorways.

So steep was the banking that the builders and subsequent maintenance gangs were unable to stand upright on it unaided, and they had to be roped up to the rim to carry out their tasks.

At that first-ever motorcycle meeting at the Surrey venue there was only one event, and the winner had the choice of claiming 20 gold sovereigns or

Brooklands programme from 1910.

George Tuttey (New Imperial) in the early years of Brooklands.

a cup. The eventual victor was W. Cook (7–9hp NLG-Peugeot), followed by E. Kickham (7hp Leader-Peugeot) and C.R. (Charlie) Collier (6hp Matchless-JAP). The winner averaged 63mph (101km/h).

Interestingly, many riders taking part also created new speed records. For example, W. Cook, the winner of the first motorcycle race at Brooklands became the first holder of the world speed record when he covered the flying kilometre (one-way) at an event in 1909 at almost 76mph (122km/h).

In 1911 the celebrated American champion, Jake de Rosier (Indian), came over to Brooklands and set a new record speed of 85.38mph (137.37km/h). It was Charlie Collier who emerged as de Rosiers's biggest rival, with Charlie being determined to hold the record for Britain. In August that year the two men competed in what is generally accepted as probably the most thrilling match races ever seen at Brooklands. No records were actually broken, though de Rosier succeeded in winning two of the three races. Before leaving England, de Rosier succeeded in putting the record up again to 88.87mph (142.99km/h). The Colliers (the owners of the London-based Matchless factory) entertained the American to a farewell dinner, and then shortly afterwards went down to Brooklands where Charlie proceeded to hoist the flying kilometre to 89.48mph (143.97km/h) and the flying mile to 91.37mph (147.01km/h)!

After World War One, fresh champions arose at Brooklands. Before the conflict, O.C. Godfrey, Victor Surridge, G.E. Stanley, J.R. Haswell and the Collier brothers had been the top names. But in the decade following the war a whole new set of names came on to the scene. These included Victor Horsman (eight times holder of the One Hour Record between 1920 and 1926), Major F.B. Halford, George Denley (the first man to top the magic 'ton'), Freddie Dixon, Bill Lacey, Herbert Le Vack, C.F. Temple, O.M. Baldwin, Wal Phillips, Daniel O'Donovan, Rex Judd and Wal Handley to name but a few.

In April 1921 D.H. Davidson (Harley-Davidson) became the first man in history to cover the kilometre one-way at over 100mph (actually 100.76mph – 162.12km/h). Then both Temple and Le Vack tore down to Brooklands to begin their own attempts. By the end, Le Vack (riding a 10-year-old eight-valve Indian v-twin) had upped the record to 106.52mph (171.39km/h).

However, by now Brooklands was becoming less suitable for record-breaking, and the last man to break the kilometre record at the Surrey speed bowl was C.F. Temple (British Anzani), when in November 1923 he clocked 108.48mph (174.54km/h). From then on the record-breakers went to continental Europe to set new speeds.

The last time the One Hour world record was taken at Brooklands was in 1928, when Bill Lacey (Grindley-Pearless-JAP) set a new record at 103.3mph (166.2km/h).

Even though the world speed record-breakers had departed, racing still continued apace at Brooklands, and in 1929 Joe Wright (Zenith-JAP) pushed the lap record to 117mph (188km/h).

In 1930 *The Motor Cycle* staged what it described as a 'giant party' to celebrate the BMCRC's (British Motor Cycle Racing Club) 21st anniversary. Expecting thousands, actually tens of thousands turned up. The track authorities were simply overwhelmed and the crowd numbers, the highest ever seen in Brooklands history, queued for miles. This meeting was the forerunner of an annual Clubman's Day at the Surrey track – a feature throughout the 1930s.

The decade before World War Two saw many new names pushing their way to Brooklands and beyond-Brooklands stardom. These included the great Eric Fernihough (who died in Hungary during 1938 trying to regain the maximum speed record for Britain), L.J. (Les) Archer, C.B. Bicknell, Johnny Lockett, Ted Barawanath, Ivor Wickstead, Ron Harris, David Whitworth, Jock West, Charles Mortimer Snr, Harold Daniell and Noel Pope.

In 1937 the Campbell circuit was opened to provide something closer to road racing conditions than the track had provided hitherto. Measuring some 2.25 miles (3.62km) per lap, it consisted of a road cutting across the centre of the course from the middle of the Railway Straight to the Fort, where it crossed the Finishing Straight and ran parallel to it to the foot of the Test Hill, where a hairpin brought it back through the Public Enclosure to the beginning of the Member's Banking.

Programme from
6 September 1930.

An evocative picture of Chas Mortimer Snr at Brooklands in the mid-1930s. The machine is not a 'Manx' Norton but instead an early 1930s International purchased for the sum of £25!

Brooklands programme from 31 August 1935.

Crystal Palace programme and map from 1928.

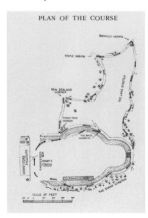

Riding a supercharged 996cc Brough Superior, Pope set a new, and as it turned out final, Brooklands motorcycle lap record at 125mph (201.12km/h) in July 1939.

Finally, as *The Motor Cycle* commented in 1946, 'Brooklands has been in existence for nearly 40 years. It was a cradle of aviation. It saw the first, feeble flights of the early aeronauts in their flimsy, pterodactyl-like craft. It was always a home of speed. It has stimulated the search for high-speed efficiency in motorcycle and car. Now the aircraft interests have won. It seems a great pity.'

On a happier note, enthusiasts are today able to visit Brooklands, and even though the vast majority of the 2.75-mile (4.42km) concrete track is no more, it is still possible to recapture just what made Brooklands so great. One can only hope this remains so for future generations, as this is a truly historic venue. In April 2008 a celebration was held at the venue to celebrate the 100 years since that first motorcycle event at the circuit.

CRYSTAL PALACE

Situated in south-east London, the story of motorcycle racing at Crystal Palace began in 1926 when a group of enthusiasts led by F.E. Mockford and L.C. Smith approached the Crystal Palace trustees in the name of London Motor Sports Ltd to see if the grounds of the Palace could provide a venue for motorcycle racing in the London area. Their dream was realised, and the first meeting (path, rather than tarmac) was held one gloriously hot sunny day on 21 May 1927 with a crowd of over 10,000 spectators.

These paths ran through parkland which had surrounded the Crystal Palace, a vast glass building (hence the name) that had stood in Hyde Park for the Great Exhibition in 1851 and was subsequently dismantled and moved to be rebuilt at Sydenham (and was finally destroyed by fire in 1936).

Two further meetings were held in 1927, on 6 August before a crowd of 15,000, and on 17 September with over 17,000 people present, both again in perfect weather. The outright lap record at the end of 1927 was held by Gus Kuhn (later to become a well-known London motorcycle dealership).

There were two meetings in 1928 but only one in 1929. In the latter, even though it rained throughout the day, another famous name, Harold Daniell, set a new lap record.

A reason for less meetings had been the arrival of speedway, with a nearly oval circuit being constructed. From a small start, speedway took off at Crystal Palace, reaching its peak in the years 1930–32. And in fact a Test match between England and Australia was staged at the venue on 27 June

1931, which was won by England. However, by the end of 1933, motorcycle speedway had ceased at the Palace, with motor car speedway taking over for the 1934 season.

In the meantime, an attempt had been made to bring back motorcycle racing over the existing paths and roads. The Streatham and District MCC organised a revival meeting on 28 October 1933. Harold Daniell and Jack Surtees (father of John) were the solo and sidecar stars respectively. Three further meetings were staged in 1934.

Then in 1936 came news of a new organisation, the International Road Racing Club, and a new circuit, designed by C.L. Clayton, a notable architect. Measuring two miles (3.2km) in length, the tarmaced track held its first motorcycle meeting, the Coronation Grand Prix, on 15 May 1937. In the three seasons before the outbreak of World War Two many of the country's top stars raced at the Palace, including Harold Daniell, Jock West, Stanley Woods, Ted Mellors, Noel Pope and Jack Surtees.

The first post-war motorcycle race meeting took place on 27 June 1953, but the circuit's length had been reduced to 1.39 miles (2.23km). When the Crystal Palace grounds were eventually cleared of debris resulting from their wartime function, the property was acquired by the London County Council in 1951. The inner loop of the pre-war circuit had been bypassed by the construction of a sweeping 1:8 downhill section joining Park Curve (near the lake) with the finishing straight.

Programme and map from 1937.

Sydenham Cup race, 1938. J. Upton (Norton) is leading. Note the hazardous concrete barrier.

Advert from 1957.

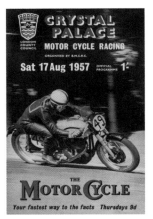

Programme from 1957.

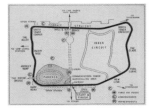

1957 map showing the new track after the circuit length had been reduced.

At that first meeting Maurice Cann (Moto Guzzi) won the 250cc final, with Bob Keeler (Norton) victorious in both the 350 and 1000cc classes and Pip Harris (Norton) taking the sidecar honours.

It was to be a certain John Surtees who became the first post-war 'King of the Palace'. By the end of 1954, John held all the major solo-lap and race records. That season his superb riding ability and meteoric starts saw him notch up no less than 31 wins in a single season – a feat never to be bettered at the south London circuit.

At the Easter meeting of 1955, over 30,000 packed the circuit. A year later, the crowd was even bigger, with John Surtees bringing the four-cylinder MV Agusta to the Palace. In 1957 Surtees (riding his own Manx Norton) set a new lap record at 79.43mph (127.8km/h). Everyone now thought the 80mph (128.7km/h) figure would be exceeded soon; however, it was in fact nearly seven years before Joe Dunphy (also Norton-mounted) finally bettered it by a small margin.

The 1958 season produced a vintage crop of budding stars, with names such as Derek Minter, Joe Dunphy and Phil Read all making their presence felt, together with a certain S.M.B. Hailwood. Interestingly, Mike was destined to become the only competitor to have held both a motorcycle and car lap record at the circuit.

With the arrival of the 1960s, work began on the construction of the new National Sports Centre, and as a consequence the paddock, start and finish were relocated from along the bottom straight to their definitive site in 1960. This also saw the removal of the controversial Ramp Bend (which was the scene of a much-publicised fatal crash) and its railway sleepers. Although the safety might have improved, the standard of racing did not quite match that of the 1950s. Joe Dunphy's lap record lasted until 1968, when Paul Smart (Curley Norton), the first of a new generation of emerging stars at the circuit, fractionally raised it to 80.45mph (129.44km/h).

From the late 1960s names such as Ray Pickrell, Peter Williams, Pat Mahoney, Barry Ditchburn and Dave Potter all began to appear in the Palace results.

In 1970 Paul Smart incredibly established six new lap and race records in a single meeting, a feat not seen since the Surtees era, and in September that year he pushed his Triumph 750 triple round to a new lap record of 84.53mph (136km/h).

In May 1972 the Greater London Council's Arts and Recreation Committee decided to close the circuit to racing at the end of the season. The desire of the National Sports Centre to expand, noise pollution and the cost of improving spectator facilities, as well as bringing the circuit up to international standards, were among the official reasons given for the decision.

GOODWOOD

Although Goodwood is more well known as a car circuit, it was once used for motorcycles in the early 1950s, while today cars and motorcycles take part annually in the Goodwood Revival Meeting, usually staged in September.

A month after Silverstone opened, another wartime airfield (Goodwood) was unveiled for racing. This was at Westhampnett in West Sussex. This had been a vital satellite base for the famous Battle of Britain fighter aerodrome. Situated at the foot of the South Downs, it took its name from the nearby stately home of the Duke of Richmond and Gordon (an enthusiastic motorcyclist who used to race ABC machines) and the racecourse perched high in the chalky hills above.

Opened in July 1948, the first car meeting was staged by the Junior Car Club on Saturday 18 September that year, but it was not until February 1951 that first news came of a motorcycle meeting. To be organised by the BMCRC, it was scheduled for 14 April and was of national status.

Measuring 2.38 miles (3.82km), the circuit comprised much of the original airfield perimeter track but, even so, abounded in very fast, sweeping bends, plus the tighter Lavant and Woodcote sections and the Chicane just before the start and finish line.

As for the April 1951 meeting, this had attracted a star-studded field, including Geoff Duke, Dickie Dale, Johnny Lockett, George Brown, Ken Kavanagh, Bill Doran and Mick Featherstone, plus Maurice Cann, Cecil Sandford and Roland Pike on 250cc machines; Bill Boddice was the top sidecar exponent.

Programme and map from 1937.

Rare unpublished photograph showing the Goodwood paddock as it was on 14 April 1951.

The field get under way in a special race for AJS 7R machines at Goodwood, 14 April 1951.

Not only did Duke win both the 350 and 500cc races on his factory Nortons, but he also set the fastest lap (and the course record for motorcycles) at 89.1mph (143.3km/h).

Quite why motorcycle racing did not return to the original Goodwood circuit is something of a mystery, however, in the car world there were to be a number of serious accidents, including one which ended Stirling Moss's career in 1962, while eight years later Bruce McLaren died while testing one of his own cars.

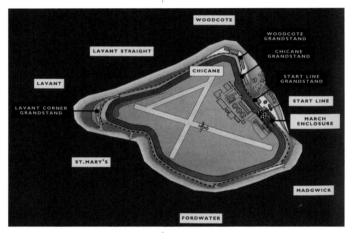

Goodwood now hosts a series of Revival meetings, where even the spectators are encouraged to wear period dress.

Eventually even the cars left, and Goodwood became a test track – a role which it continued until the end of 1997, before work began on a total renovation, funded by the current owner, Lord March. This revival of the circuit brought Goodwood back to life, with many of the drivers and riders of yesteryear taking part in historic races and parades. Even spectators are encouraged to wear period dress, as each year Goodwood becomes what the organisers call 'a time capsule for three days of spectacular entertainment.'

GRANDSDEN LODGE

In June 1946, the Cambridge University AC held its first race meeting since World War Two at Grandsden Lodge Airfield, the base being situated two miles from Caxton, on the main Royston to Huntingdon road. As with other similar meetings at the time (for example North Weald a week later), the proceeds were going to the RAF fund for St Dunstans.

The circuit, measuring 2.15 miles (3.45km) and in the shape of a triangle, using two runways and part of the perimeter road, was of tarmacadam offering what one observer said was 'excellent wheelgrip – wet or dry'.

Competitors had a large enclosed hanger as a paddock, with the perimeter road nearby for warming up engines. The stewards were able to assemble riders and send them to the start line via the perimeter road while the preceding race was in progress. It was a combined motorcycle and car meeting, there being four motorcycle events. The 250cc event was won by G. Newman (Rudge) with Ray Petty (New Imperial) and Doug Beasley (Excelsior) second and third. Peter Goodman (of the Goodman family, owners of the Veloce company, the makers of Velocette machines) was victorious in the 350cc event – on a Velo of course! In both the 500cc and Unlimited races Sid Barnett (Norton) came out on top followed by George Brown (Vincent HRD) and Eric Briggs (Norton).

LONG MARSTON

During the 1950s and 1960s Long Marston, Hertfordshire was well-known in motorcycle sporting circles for sprint event, with such famous riders as George Brown, Charlie Rous and Basil Keys. Then during the 1970s it was used as a road racing circuit. Track length unknown.

LYDDEN HILL

At the beginning of 1965 Derek Minter received an invitation, via *Motor Cycling,* to give Britain's newest circuit, Lydden Hill, near Canterbury in Kent, the once-over. After some 50 laps on his works Cotton and his own 350 Norton, Derek pronounced the course 'OK'.

Also at the test session was Sittingbourne businessman Bill Cheeson who had been involved with events at Lydden since 1955, and advisor to the circuit owner, William Mark Holdings Ltd. Lydden, already well known for grass track events organised by the Astro club, was also a former scrambles circuit with the newly tarmaced road racing course measuring just under one mile (1.61km).

After lapping in both directions, Derek opted for a clockwise circuit. That way, he said, it 'would be faster, safer for the riders and more interesting for the spectators.' So that's the way it was and still is today.

The first meeting at Lydden took place on Sunday 4 April 1965. It was Charlie Sanby who was the undisputed star of that first meeting and who was later to win the 'Lord of Lydden' title.

In 1967 the circuit began Rallycross using a combined tarmac and dirt track becoming well known to the public via the TV coverage of the meetings, and a much-repeated 'gaffe' by Murray Walker.

As I know from personal experience, Lydden Hill is a particularly tight, demanding track. In fact, when riding in the very last 50cc Enduro in 1972, I felt it was an ideal circuit for these small machines – as, even with so miniscule a machine, one was 'laid over' a lot of the time.

In 1989 the circuit was sold to Rallycross enthusiast Tom Bisset, after which the TAG-McClaren organisation took a 50 per cent share in Lydden.

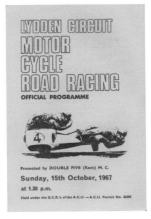

Early Lydden programme from 1967.

Lydden programme and
map from 2008.

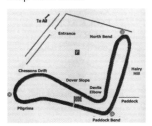

Bisset was forced to sell his share of the venue in 1991, resulting in TAG-McClaren becoming the sole owner. Originally, the TAG-McClaren group had plans to turn Lydden into a Formula One test track, then a road car test track, but all these plans were eventually axed. Without a club based at the circuit or an organisation to run it, racing ceased for a period of nine months.

In 1993 McClaren reached an agreement with the British Motor Cycle Racing Club (BMCRC), the latter being given a lease to manage the circuit for a five-year period from 1994 onwards. In 1996 there were several safety improvements, with the moving back of the tyre wall and extension of gravel traps at Paddock Bend, Devil's Elbow and the Hairpin.

Since the beginning of the 21st century, however, the circuit has faced an uncertain future, and thus development has been restricted. Even so, as this book is being written Lydden Hill remains an active circuit. A particularly popular annual motorcycle event is the meeting run by the Classic Racing Motorcycle Club.

NORTH WEALD

The headline in *The Motor Cycle* dated 27 June 1946 said it all, 'Road Racing Thanks to the RAF'. The report began, 'An airfield, for all its perimeter roads, may not be the Isle of Man, or even Donington, but, ye gods, what the road racing at North Weald meant to London enthusiasts last Saturday. Shades of Brooklands on *The Motor Cycle's* Clubman's Day.' Anyway, the attending crowd could only be described as vast. The meeting, organised by the Wood Green club in conjunction with the St Dunstan's Appeal Committee of the RAF, was superbly organised. Not only did the whole affair run smoothly, with RAF personnel helping, but the police as well. As *The Motor Cycle* reported, 'there was all the atmosphere of a big road race meeting, with facilities second to none. Picture a "roadway" an airfield runway – 150ft wide as the competitors' park and half a mile or so more of it for competitors to use to their heart's content for checking off the state of their mounts and for warming them up. There was the smell of "R", the reek of dope fuels, the music of racing exhausts, and warm weather with not a drop of rain.'

From a spectator's point of view, there was what was described as 'a resemblance of Brooklands in that the vastness tended to diminish the impression of speed.' Some 3.2 miles (5.14km) long, the circuit was made more difficult for the riders because of its great width. As for the races themselves, Harold Daniell (then the holder of the TT lap record) won the Unlimited Solo race on his Norton, while David Whitworth (Velocette) was the 350cc victor; there was even a novice race. Everyone agreed it had been a brilliant day when the last event ended at 7.15 that evening. It was to be a one-off for this particular circuit, but a great one nonetheless.

PADDINGTON

Motorcycle racing came to the heart of London on Friday evening, 17 August 1962, when the New Era 50cc Racing Club presented a meeting on the banked cycle track in the Paddington Recreation Grounds at Randolph Avenue. The local council said they were keen to stage this type of event regularly, and the circuit had been given the green light by the ACU – for 50cc events only.

The circuit was some 0.4 miles (0.64km) in length, with the fastest riders lapping at around 48mph (77.23km/h). Unfortunately the meeting suffered from a lack of entries (only 14), and a combination of non-starters and mechanical failure meant the evening was not much of a success.

SCULTHORPE

Sculthorpe, near Fakenham in West Norfolk, was an American Airforce base during the 1950s and 1960s. It then came under the care and maintenance of the RAF.

The Newmarket and District MCC and LCC held a number of successful meetings at Snetterton from the early 1970s and into the 1980s. However, with the arrival of the Nicola Foulston regime at Brands Hatch (the owners of Snetterton), circuit hire cost rose dramatically at the beginning of the 1990s. This saw the demise of many smaller clubs as regards road racing. Newmarket and its chairman David Bailey were not to be one of them as they moved to Sculthorpe. This was a typical airfield circuit of the type found in the immediate post-World War Two era, with little in the way of facilities but an ability to provide racing at a low cost thanks to the co-operation of the RAF. The circuit utilised existing tarmac and measured some one and a half miles (2.41km) in length; running clockwise in direction.

Meetings ceased there due in a great part to the illness and subsequent death of David Bailey during the mid-1990s.

SNETTERTON

The brainchild of Oliver Sear (to which Sear's Corner is a permanent reminder), Snetterton was a former United States Army Air Force base during World War Two. It opened for cars in the autumn of 1951. Situated

The famous Bombhole in its original guise, 10 October 1955. The rider is John Surtees (247cc NSU Sportmax).

Peter Darvill (750 Honda) on the Start/Finish straight leads Tony Spencer (750 Chat Yam) and Geoff Barry (750 Oakley Commando), Snetterton, 30 August 1970.

some 18 miles (29km) south west of Norwich, first news of Snetterton as a motorcycle venue came early in 1953. Measuring 2.7 miles (4.3km) in length at this time, the lap included a hairpin bend and several left and right-hand bends.

Dates that first year were 2 May and 5 September. The first of these was open-to-Eastern-Centre and the organisers were called the Snetterton Combine, which comprised those clubs in Norfolk, Suffolk and Essex. The first secretary was R.J. (Bob) Havers of Norwich. Many of the sections of that original circuit remain, notably Riches (the first corner after the start), Sears, The Esses, The Bombhole and Coram.

In that very first motorcycle race meeting at Snetterton on May 1953 John Surtees (Nortons) was victorious in both the 350 and 500cc events. Other winners were John Hogan in the 125cc (BSA) and Maurice Cann in the 250cc race (Moto Guzzi), while Bill Boddice and Ted Davis had shared the sidecar honours on Norton and Vincent machinery respectively.

Up to 1975 there was the famous one-mile (1.6km) Norwich Straight with its hairpin, but this section was removed due to the Opec oil price rises of the mid-1970s and a much shorter connecting straight (named after Geoff Revett the former Ipswich motorcycle dealer) incorporated.

Russell's (named after the Jim Russell Racing School, which for many years had its base at Snetterton) between Coram and the start came into being at the beginning of the 1966 season and must rate as the most altered corner in circuit history. Introduced to slow cars rather than bikes, it proved more akin to a skid pan than a corner, and after many crashes – from Mike Hailwood to the author – it was changed at the end of that year. Since then it has been altered on

several occasion and now seems to have found the definitive line, but this does not stop yet more crashes there every season. The post-1975 circuit length is 1.952 miles (3.141km).

Since the 1960s Snetterton has been associated with the various owners of Brands Hatch, currently controlled by Jonathan Palmer. As for Oliver Sear, he resigned as managing director of Snetterton at the end of February 1965. Although by then already part of the Grovewood Securities Group, Snetterton, like Oulton Park, had been controlled independently up to that time.

An interesting and little-known fact is that in 1990 the then owner Nicola Foulston attempted to turn Snetterton into a major housing development. The circuit was saved by the leasehold of the Snetterton Market, which occupies the former Norwich Straight and Hairpin sections.

Many famous riders have appeared at Snetterton over the years, and today it hosts a round of the British Superbike series each year. It has also proved a popular venue for endurance racing and testing, as well as hosting the Transatlantic Trophy series during the 1970s and early 1980s.

Finally an incident in 1972 helped change what was an outmoded practice – that of allowing cars and bikes out together in testing. Emerson Fitapaldi was circling together with a number of bikes including a certain person (I will refrain from naming him) on a racing BSA Bantam. Fitapaldi caught the Bantam rider up in the middle of the Bombhole and put tyre marks down the side of the Bantam's fairing. Needless to say, said rider came back into the pits with a white face and needing a quick change of underwear!

Who could have known then that Snetterton was still to be an important circuit for both motorcycles and cars all these years later? No doubt Oliver Sear would have been proud, for it was to this man that the father of Snetterton title should be awarded.

STAPLEFORD TAWNEY

During early 1947 the North East London MC obtained permission to hold a race meeting on Saturday 12 April that year at Stapleford Tawney airfield, on the Abridge-Ongar road in Essex.

The circuit had a tarmac surface, was just over two miles (3.2km) in length and abounded in curves and bends. There was a considerable rise between the start and the back of the course, and as with many such events during the immediate post-war period (in this case The Army Benevolent Fund) the proceeds were destined for charity.

Most of the regular short circuit riders were in attendance at that first meeting, including the likes of Denis Parkinson, Geoff Monty, Roland Pike

Programme from 1984.

The Snetterton circuit in 1997.

Programme from 2008.

Stapleford Tawney airfield circuit programme and map from 1947.

The programme from the 1977 race meeting at Thorney Island.

and Tommy Woods, a major disappointment being that Les Graham was a non-starter after his 500 pushrod AJS broke a valve spring. Thousands of spectators saw Johnny Lockett win two races and in the process lap at over 67mph (107.8km/h).

Another excellent meeting was staged in August 1947, this time in aid of the Agricultural Disaster Fund. So large was the entry that the club had to ballot would-be starters, and those whose names failed to come out of the hat were to be disappointed! Even so, the programme numbered some 130 riders, including such well-known names as Maurice Cann, Eric Oliver, Frank Fry, George Brown and Cyril Smith – to add to the stars who attended the April meeting. This time the main race, the 1000cc final, was won by Maurice Cann (Moto Guzzi).

Sadly, this venue was to be available for only a single season, but for those two meetings Stapleford Tawney proved popular with both riders and spectators alike.

THORNEY ISLAND

Organised jointly by the Southampton & District MCC and the RAFMSA (Royal Air Force Motor Sports Association), the race meeting at Thorney Island, West Sussex, took place on Sunday 11 September 1977. Interestingly, former racer and well-known Special builder, Len Harfield, was the chief scrutineer that day. The public were requested 'not to wander around the Ministry of Defence buildings, and to confine themselves to the vicinity of the circuit.'

Among the entry were Fred Launchbury, Basil Keys, Rob Marks, Tony Godfrey, Steve Bateman, Fred Huggett and Barry Seward.

WATERBEACH

The inaugural Waterbeach road races were held on Sunday 19 October 1975, organised by the Newmarket and District MCC & LCC. The circuit, on the site of an existing RAF airfield (later taken over by the army) had a length of around one and a half miles (2.4km). From the start riders proceeded to Abbey and then Crossways (both fast curves), then to the much sharper Willows, followed by Esses One and Esses Two with Runway One leading out onto the main straight (making up approximately a third of the circuit length). Then came the Chicane, followed by the Hairpin and so back to the start line. The meeting was blessed by a large entry, with reserves for many races. Besides the author's two entries (Manx GP winner Dave Arnold and Ian Gittins), other riders included Jeff Crookbain, Dave Cartwright, Greg Page, Gordon Russell, Roger Winterburn, Leigh Notman, Dennis Trollope and Ray Knight.

WELWYN GARDEN CITY

Claimed to have been the first motorcycle race meeting on a banked track in Britain since Brooklands closed in 1939, this was held at the Gosling Stadium, Welwyn Garden City in Hertfordshire, on Saturday 14 April 1962. Cold weather and lack of prior publicity kept the number of spectators to a minimum, but the standard of racing – organised exclusively for 50cc machines by the Racing 50 MCC – was excellent. Riders included Mike Simmonds, Charlie Mates, Bill Ivy, Phil Horsham, Beryl Swain and Brian Brader.

Normally used for cycle racing, the fastest 50cc riders were lapping the circuit at over 60mph (96.5km/h). The circuit was, in effect, a 0.3-mile (0.48km) tarmac bowl.

Programme of the 1975 Waterbeach road races.

West Raynham 26 July 1987, Forgotten Era club meeting, Neil Chilton (492cc Suzuki).

The open expanse of RAF station West Raynham, c.1987.

WEST RAYNHAM

West Raynham was a Royal Air Force station some four miles (6.5km) south west of the Norfolk market town of Fakenham and was used for racing from the late 1970s and much of the following decade. It was a typical airfield circuit and meetings were run here by the Newmarket and District club.

SOUTH WEST

Blandford (1948–60)

Bryanston Park (1947)

Castle Combe (1951–)

Chivenor (2000)

Colerne (late 1970s–early 1980s)

Goram Fair (1959)

Ibsley (1951–53)

Imber Road (1948–53)

Keevil (late 1970s, early 1980s)

Little Rissington (1964–66)

Moreton Valance (late 1960s)

Pendennis Castle (1930s)

Plymouth (1938)

Staverton (1969–mid-1970s)

St Eval (1966–67)

Sutton Veney (1950)

Thruxton (1950–64, 1968–)

Weston-super-Mare (1949)

Wroughton (1970s)

Wymering Park (1930s)

BLANDFORD

Blandford Camp in Dorset had its first motorcycle road race meeting one lovely summer's day in late July 1948. Immediately it was acclaimed as a circuit which could, potentially, host racing at the highest level. This first meeting, as were so many at the time, was organised to aid charities – in this case a combination of army regimental ones and the British Legion. The meeting's organisers were the Blackmore Vale Club.

Measuring some 3.2-miles (5.1km) in length, in shape the course was roughly rectangular and ran in a clockwise direction. The start and finish were in the middle of a straight just under 0.5 miles (0.8km) in length. Then came Cuckoo Corner, a right-hand 90-degree turn with a slight adverse camber, followed by a very fast downhill sweep. Then it ran in a different direction and up a steady incline to the hutted REME camp. A right-angle turn, Anson Corner, with a rounded apex lay in the camp itself. This was followed by a series of very fast bends to a deceptive right-hand bend,

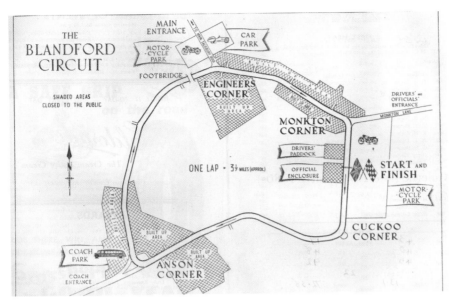

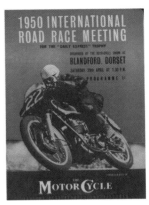

The Blandford Camp map from a 1950 programme.

Engineers Corner, at the entry to a second camp, that of the RASC. Finally, there was a sharp right-hand turn into the finishing straight.

There was riding talent aplenty at that first meeting with 250, 350, 500cc and clubman's races. Bob Foster was the star that day, winning the 350cc (Velocette) and 500cc (Triumph) events. Other riders included Maurice Cann (who won the 250cc race), Sid Barnett, Noel Pope, Roland Pike and Les Graham. Foster set the fastest lap of the day at 85.9mph (138.2km/h).

In contrast, the second meeting of 1948, in mid-October, saw torrential rain, which transformed the circuit to one demanding great respect. Les Graham (AJS) won both the main races, but lap times were well down.

The third meeting, held in April 1949, saw several new names coming to Blandford, including a certain young G.E. (Geoff) Duke, Johnny Lockett and Harold Daniell on factory Nortons. Even so, Les Graham again was victorious in the 350 and 500cc finals. Two more meetings were held at Blandford in 1949 in August and September. At the end of that year came the first news that the ACU planned to hold an international meeting on 29 April 1950.

It was at this event that Geoff Duke gave the works McCandless Featherbed Norton its racing debut and in the process won the 500cc race witnessed by a crowd well in excess of 40,000. There were two fatalities, however, and this was to cause the authorities to suspend racing after the 1950 August Bank Holiday meeting, at which Geoff Duke had set a new course lap record of 88.95mph (143.12km/h).

After the circuit was resurfaced, racing resumed there on Whit Monday 1951. Even so, a St John's Ambulance man and a spectator were injured when two riders collided, adding to the circuit's safety issues.

Blandford Camp, 350cc
final, Easter Monday 1954.
41 Bob Gerrard (Norton), 43
Maurice Quincey (Norton),
77 Derek Farrant (AJS).

1953 programme.

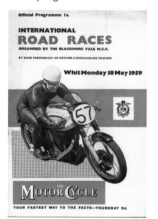

1959 programme.

1960 programme.

Although the meeting scheduled for April 1952 was cancelled, Blandford did host one other that year – the last British race meeting of the year in mid-October – with John Surtees taking his 499cc Norton to victory in the 500cc and Invitation events.

The fourth international road race meeting at Blandford on August Bank Holiday Monday 1953 was notable because all four lap records were broken. Besides John Surtees, other interesting entries included Fergus Anderson and Bob McIntyre.

In May 1959 Derek Minter set a new lap record of 92.21mph (148.36km/h) on his 499cc Lancefield Norton; he also broke the 350cc record at 90.15mph (145.05km/h).

The final Blandford meeting came a year later, at the beginning of June 1960, but although there was a large entry Minter's records remained untouched. For the first time since 1951 there was a sidecar race, which was won by the German star Helmut Fath (BMW).

Then at the Blackmore Vale Club's annual dinner in December that year the sad news was announced that there would be no more racing as Blandford Camp, through which the circuit ran, was to be expanded and would no longer be available. Therefore, for 1961 the club transferred to Thruxton in Hampshire.

BRYANSTON PARK

Bryanston Park in Blandford, Dorset can best be described as a 'makeshift course'. Why? Well, the organising Blackmore Vale Club had arranged a meeting at another venue, only to be informed a week before the event, that their chosen course could not be used on a Sunday. What were they to do? Scrap the event or use another circuit. In an attempt to avoid disappointing the 55 entries, the latter course of action was adopted.

Practising took place on the evening of Saturday 10 May 1947 on a circuit which some said was more suitable for trials tyres than racing rubber. There were many tall trees in Bryanston Park, providing an unusual setting for a speed event. But on the following day the 350cc race in particular was hotly contested, with Tommy Wood taking victory from Peter Goodman and Allan Dudley-Ward (all on Velocettes). In the 250cc event Roland Pike won on his Rudge, while Johnny Lockett was victorious on his Norton in the 500cc tussle.

As for the course itself. After a short straight there was a left-hand S-bend. This was followed by a 90-degree right turn, a sweep left and then a turn off the road on to a dry, dusty 'cart track', as one report called it. This track led downhill to a right-hand hairpin, which caused considerable problems for competitors. After this came a tarmac road, just before right-left-right bends, uphill, leading to the finishing straight. The distance was approximately one and a half miles (2.4km).

The Blackmore Vale Club said it hoped to improve this circuit by tarring the entire track, but this did not happen.

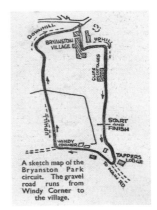

A sketch map of the Bryanston Park circuit. The gravel road runs from Windy Corner to the village.

Bryanston Park, 1947.

CASTLE COMBE

The first-ever motorcycle race meeting over Wiltshire's Castle Combe circuit, former RAF wartime airfield (1940–46), took place on Saturday 28 July 1951. Near Chippenham, the 1.84-mile (2.96km) course ran in a clockwise direction. From the starting line the track led via one right-hand and one left-hand bend into a hairpin at Quarry Corner. Farm Straight was next, through two gentle bends, to the sharp Tower Corner. A long straight (Dean) took the course to Camp Corner and then back to the start. Even in those days the 'Combe' was known for its fast but bumpy nature.

The Bristol Motor Cycle and Light Car Club was the organisation that can be accredited with getting the circuit off the ground. A fair spattering of well-known racing names appeared in that first meeting's programme, including Syd Lawton, Ray Petty, George Todd, Jack Difazio, Robin Sherry, Basil Keys, John Surtees, Geoff Monty, Bob Foster, Pip Harris, Cyril Smith, Jack Surtees and Bill Boddice. The winners were 125cc John Hogan, 250 and 350cc Robin Sherry, 500cc H.L. Williams, and sidecars Pip Harris.

Next, on 6 September 1952, the first national motorcycle event at the new circuit saw the Bristol club join forces with the Wessex Centre ACU to put on a more high-profile event. Besides many of the original riders,

Castle Combe programme, 1951.

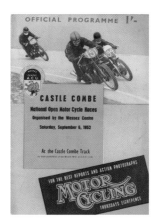

1952 programme.

Castle Combe programme
and map from 1960.

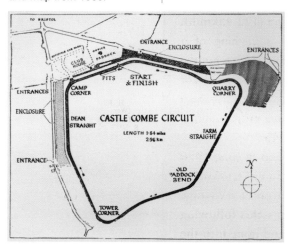

newcomers included Brian Setchell, Ginger Payne, Bob Keeler, P.H. Carter, Allan Dudley-Ward, Maurice Cann, Denis Lashmar and Sid Barnett.

In the early days John Surtees was very much the star at Castle Combe, and he held many of the lap records. A particularly successful day was 9 July 1955, when he won not only the 250, 350 and 500cc races, but also set new class lap records in the 250cc at 78.11mph (125.67km/h) on his NSU and 350cc at 82.59mph (132.88km/h) on his Norton.

From 1956 until 1961 no car racing took place at Castle Combe. In July 1957 the Scot Alastair King lapped at 85.79mph (138.03km/h) to establish a new outright motorcycle lap record at the Wiltshire circuit, where bikes were the sole form of revenue at the time.

Interestingly, the King of Brands, Derek Minter, proved to be almost as successful at the Combe, often beating all the top men from 1958, including even Mike Hailwood in the larger classes. Other notable riders of this era included Dan Shorey, Tony Godfrey and Phil Read.

Unlike many circuits, Castle Combe remained true to its original form, and so lap records meant actual riding/machine improvements, although AFN took over the lease at the end of 1963 and their first act was to totally resurface the track early the following year.

By 1966 the class lap records were as follows:

50cc	Dave Simmonds (Tohatsu)	72.79mph (117.11km/h)
125cc	Bill Ivy (Honda)	82.59mph (132.88km/h)
250cc	Dave Simmonds (Honda)	86.93mph (139.87km/h)
350cc	Derek Minter (Norton)	89.27mph (139.87km/h)
500cc	Derek Minter (Norton)	91.75mph (143.63km/h)
Sidecars	Bill Boddice (Norton)	86.25mph (138.77km/h)

In 1965 the circuit had seen, for one year only, the running of the 500-mile (805km) endurance race for production machines, won by Dave Degens and Barry Lawton riding Syd Lawton's 649cc Triumph Bonneville.

The track needed resurfacing again at the end of the 1966 season, which begs the question, why had the resurfacing of only three years earlier not lasted longer? There were also problems with both planning permission (always ongoing during the 1950s and 1960s) and extension of the lease. If all this was not enough, a small number of local residents were by now complaining about noise and pollution issues. Also, the number of motorcycle meetings was cut to only two for the 1967 season, and this was not well received by the Wessex Centre ACU. This prompted a statement from them saying, 'The cars have pushed us out, AFN (Castle Combe) Ltd has forgotten who kept the circuit going from 1956 to 1964.'

In 1968 Howard Strawford arrived (initially as a club secretary) and, although primarily a car man, Howard has been the driving force at Castle Combe since the early 1970s after AFN quit the scene.

As the 1970s began, threat of closure hung over the circuit due to a series of planning wrangles. Even so, Barry Sheene and other well-known names rode there in 1970 and 1971. At the end of that year, however, there was to be no bike racing at the Combe for nine long years. But the good news was that by the end of that decade the circuit gained permanent planning permission at last.

Motorcycles returned during 1981, thanks to the North Glos MCC. National level racing returned in the 1989 season for the first time in almost 20 years as the New Era club hosted the April meeting. It was at that meeting that not only did a youthful Carl Fogarty win the main race on an RC30 Honda, but he also became the first man to lap the Wiltshire course at over 100mph (161km/h) – 102.22mph (164.5km/h) to be exact. At that same meeting Mick Boddice, passengered by Chas Birks, took their Yamaha-engined machine round at over 100mph in the Sidecar event.

A year later, in April 1990, Steve Spray (Norton Rotary) upped the two-wheel lap record to 104.81mph (168.63km/h). Spray won the Formula One event from teammate Trevor Nation, with works Kawasaki rider John Reynolds third.

For 1991, again there was a single national motorcycle event to supplement the car meetings and James Whitham (Suzuki) raised the lap record once more. In June 1992 John Reynolds raised the record yet again – the fourth time in four years – with a speed of 107.18mph (172.45km/h).

Then, at the end of that year, the circuit underwent something of a transformation. Not only was the pit lane widened and doubled in size, but the entire circuit was totally resurfaced. Other changes included the construction of spectator banks at Tower and Camp corners. The paddock area was also extensively extended, and since then there has been an ongoing programme of investment to make Castle Combe's facilities better year on year.

The annual motorcycle meeting approach continued, and in June 1996 Graham Ward (Ducati) raised the lap record to 107.86mph (173.54km/h). In December 1998 circuit revisions were unveiled, featuring two new corners, the purpose of which was to slow the cars down – this following the death of a spectator when a car had shed its wheel and gone into the

Programme from
5 September 1964.

Programme from 30 April
1966.

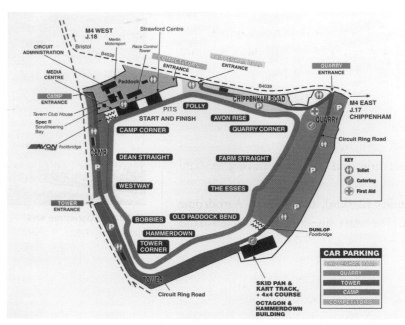

The Castle Combe circuit in 1999.

crowd at the August Bank holiday meeting. One of these new corners, named Bobbies (in memory of Bob Davies from the circuit management team who had recently passed away), was between Tower and West Way, while the other was the Esses just before Old Paddock. These changes increased the circuit length to 1.85 miles (3km).

During the 1999 season John Burgess (Yamaha) set a new lap record for the revised circuit at 94.57mph (152.16km/h).

On Saturday and Sunday 25 and 26 September 2004 Castle Combe hosted its Superbike Grand National meeting, with many of the UK's top stars, including, Michael Rutter, Steve Plater, Sean Emmett, Tommy Hill, Dean Ellison, plus the Japanese Superbike rider Ryuichi Kiyonari.

By June 2006, Castle Combe was hosting a round of Superbike and the FIM Sidecar World Championship series. And so the 'Combe' survives into the 21st century as a leading circuit for motorsport on two, three and four wheels. This is helped in no small way by the efforts of men such as Howard Strawford (chairman, Castle Combe Circuit Ltd) and track manager and former motorcycle racer Rodney Gooch.

CHIVENOR

Chivenor made its debut as a road racing circuit thanks to the North Gloucester Road Racing club, in conjunction with the Royal Air Force Motor Sports Association in 2000. Despite atrocious weather conditions, spectators flocked in to see the first ever motorcycle road race meeting to hit the North Devon coast. The track came in for one or two criticisms from the riders, but with a few circuit modifications it turned out into a well-liked venue very quickly.

As an example, at even the first meeting in the wet Seb Healy won the Open race on a 1000cc Yamaha and in the process set the fastest lap of the meeting at 83.36mph (134.12km/h).

Measuring 1.6 miles (2.57km), the Chivenor circuit ran anti-clockwise. From the start, riders had to negotiate the fast right Runaway

Chivenor programme, 2001.

Sweep, followed by left-hand Paddock Loop. Next came Camp Curve and then the Northern Hairpin. This was followed by The Esses and eventually Turn One, before exiting onto the finishing straight.

Colerne

Colerne, between Chippenham and Bath, was an airfield circuit. It was yet another to be promoted jointly by the North Gloucestershire MCC and Royal Air Force Motor Sports Association and was used during the late 1970s and early 1980s.

With a length of one and a half miles (2.4km), the Colerne Aerodrome course ran in a clockwise direction. The start line led into the left-hand Bunker Sweep. This was followed by the longest straight and Camp Curve, a right-hander. Another shorter straight led to the Hairpin, then the Loop. Next came a fast section, including, in the middle, Cadet Curve. Finally, Paddock Bend and Hanger Bend brought the riders back to the start of the lap.

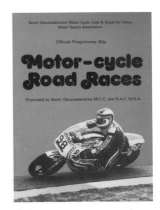

Colerne programme and map from 1980.

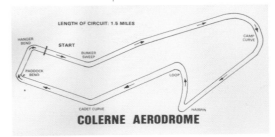

Goram Fair

In August 1959 the Bristol MCC brought road racing right onto the southern doorstep of the City of Bristol. This was restricted to Wessex Centre meeting, which had been organised with support and encouragement of the Bristol Corporation and ran over a one-mile (1.61km) circuit which surrounded the city's annual Goram Fair in the Whitchurch area of the city. It had drawn an entry of over 90 riders including Phil Read, Tom Thorp, Dan Shorey, Alan Dugdale and 'Ginger' Payne. It was Shorey (125 and

Goram Fair, 1959, with Phil Read (Manx Norton) already in the lead.

250cc) and Read (350 and 500cc) who emerged on top. The sidecar events were less clear-cut, with different winners in each of the three races.

IBSLEY

The first news that the Ringwood Club would organise airfield racing at Ibsley, near Ringwood, Hampshire, came in February 1951. The circuit had already been inspected and approved by none other than Geoff Duke, and it saw its first meeting on Saturday 12 May that year.

The circuit, essentially utilising the main runway and perimeter track, was not only very wide, but also well surfaced in tarmacadam and some 2.1 miles (3.4km) in length. The starting straight led into a sharp right-hander at Court Corner, followed by a long straight section leading to Sampson Road. There was then a gentle curve to the right into a hairpin bend at Church Corner, thereafter a straight run to Middle Road and finally another hairpin just prior to the finishing line.

The main stars at this first event were Bob Foster, Syd Lawton, Colin Horn and John Hogan with some 5,000 spectators attended.

The second Ibsley meeting ran under a national permit (the first was closed-to-centre) and there were sidecars for the first time. The solo riders included Maurice Cann, John Hogan, Geoff Monty, Michael O'Rourke, John Storr and Bob Keeler, while Pip Harris and Bill Boddice were the top three-wheelers. A new outright lap record was set by Storr (499cc Norton) at 74.55mph (119.95km/h).

The third (and final) meeting at Ibsley Airfield took place on Saturday 11 July 1953. The race winners were 125 Ivor Lloyd (MV Agusta), 250

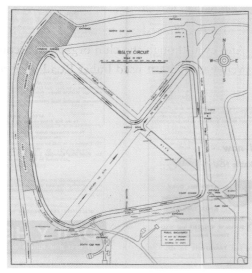

Ibsley circuit map and programme from 1954.

Maurice Cann (Moto Guzzi), 350 John Surtees (Norton) and 500cc Denis Lashmar (Pike-BSA); with sidecar Pip Harris (Norton). Due to wet conditions no lap records were broken. Other notable entries were Frank Perris and Percy Tait, both at the very beginning of their respective racing careers.

IMBER ROAD

The Wylye Valley Motor Cycle Club were responsible for running a series of road races at the army camp at Imber Road, Warminster, Wiltshire, during the late 1940s and early 1950s.

In the 0.8-mile (1.287km) circuit there was no less than 10 corners. Of these, two formed a fast S-bend and another made a wide loop or sweep to the left. The remainder were near enough 45-degree turns; the straight being short and the surface varying between tarmac and concrete. When the surface was dry it was good, but it was treacherous when wet; however, slip roads were provided and there were plenty of good, safe vantage points for spectators. The course ran anti-clockwise.

The first meeting was held in July 1948, with heats and finals for 250, 350 and 500cc solos, plus a clubman's race for production models. The 250 and 350cc races were won by Les Archer Jnr on the same EMC he won the Dunholme Hutchinson Hundred Handicap with the previous year. Archer also rode a Velocette in the 500cc final but was beaten by Brands Hatch specialist P. Maloney (Triumph).

A second meeting was staged during early October 1948 and, even though conditions were far from ideal, circuit newcomer Tommy Wood (348cc Velocette) set a new lap record. Other notable riders at this meeting included Bob Foster and Jack Difazio.

There followed one meeting in June 1949, then another on 14 May 1950. And even though the club organised a couple of meetings at nearby Sutton Veney in 1950, it used Imber Road until the end of 1953.

Imber Road programme from 1953.

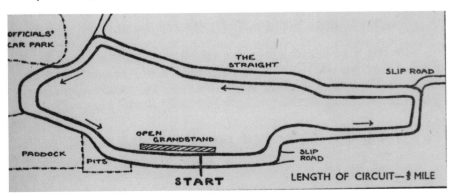

Plan of the Imber Road circuit from 1951.

Les Burgen thunders the Oxford Fairing Suzuki through the Esses at Keevil in 1981.

KEEVIL

Keevil lies between Trowbridge and Devizes in Wiltshire. Measuring 1.3 miles (2.1km) to a lap, the circuit ran in an anti-clockwise direction and was roughly triangular in shape.

The start–finish line was positioned halfway down Park Straight. The first corner that riders had to negotiate was the tight left-hand Village Turn, followed by the lengthy Nation Straight, at the end of which was the left-hand Steeple Hairpin. From there, riders accelerated into the right-hand Burnetts Bend. Next came the Esses and into the left-hand Old Paddock, which in turn led riders onto Park Straight and back to the finish line.

LITTLE RISSINGTON

Little Rissington programme, 1964.

Little Rissington, near Bourton-on-the-Water, Gloucestershire, ran two 'twisting sprints' in August and October 1963, organised by the Cheltenham Motor Club; the following year the club moved forward at the same venue by running a race meeting on Sunday 17 May 1964.

The Little Rissington circuit measured 1.15 miles (1.85km) to a lap and ran in an anti-clockwise direction. From the start and finish line competitors proceeded quickly to Hanger Bend, followed by Hanger Corner. Next came Sprint Straight, then the sharp left-hand Hairpin, followed by Copse Corner and Cottage Bend. From there was Back Straight, the fastest part of the course, at the end of which was the left-hand Peri Corner. Riders then accelerated to an un-named curve, just prior to the finish line.

As *Motor Cycle News* reported in its 20 May 1964 issue, 'Two successful and efficiently organised events run by the Cheltenham Motor Club at the

This view of Andrew French at Little Rissington in 1964 shows how loose (and dusty) the circuit was.

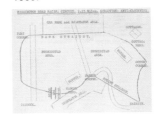

Programme and map from Little Rissington, 6 June 1965.

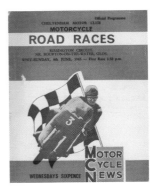

RAF station, Little Rissington, have earned even greater co-operation from the base commander this year.'

The result was that a crowd of over 11,000 watched the club's first-ever road race meeting. By bringing into use just over a mile of perimeter tracks and connecting roads, a very interesting circuit had been created, containing what *MCN* said was 'a first-class variety of bends from high-speed curves to dead-slow hairpins.'

The first final of the day was for the 125cc class, which saw a win for Jim Curry, from Rod Scivyer, Gary Dickinson and Andrew French (all on Hondas). In the 350 and 500cc finals, Welshmen Malcolm Uphill and

Paddock at Little
Rissington, summer 1965.

Moreton Valence map and
programme from 1967.

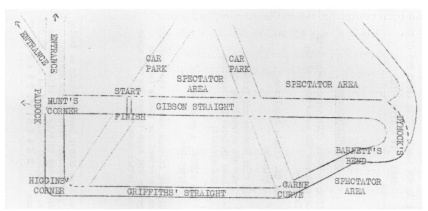

Selwyn Griffiths fought for the victory. Griffiths won the 350cc and Uphill the bigger class, while Uphill had the distinction of setting the fastest lap of the meeting on his unfaired 349cc AJS at 69.93mph (112.51km/h).

By the following year, Uphill had raised this figure to 71.13mph (114.44km/h) on a 499cc Norton.

Moreton Valence

The Cheltenham Motor Club organised a meeting at the Moreton Valance circuit near Gloucester on 24 September 1967. Like many other similar tracks, Moreton Valence made use of an airfield. Measuring 1.75 miles (2.81km) in length and running clockwise, the circuit layout consisted of Gibson Straight (which was also where the start–finish line was placed). Following this came Dymocks (essentially a sharp right-hand hairpin), followed quickly by Barnett's Bend, Garne Curve, Griffith's Straight, Higgins Corner, Hunts Corner and from there back onto Gibson Straight and the finish line.

Typical of the Cheltenham club's meetings at Moreton

Valance was the one held on Sunday 22 September 1968. It was very much a case of a father and son act – with Don Browning as the race secretary and his son, Dave, as one of the stars of the meeting. Other notable riders from the day's entry list included Ron Pladdys, Chas Mortimer, Nigel Rollason, Dennis Trollope and Richard Difazio.

Effectively, Moreton Valance replaced Little Rissington (both venues are run by the Cheltenham club).

Pendennis Castle

During the 1930s, Pendennis Castle meetings were England's only races to be held over roads normally open to the public. The course in Falmouth, Cornwall, was one and a half miles (2.41km) in length and encircled Pendennis Castle at the entrance to Falmouth Harbour. Lying on a peninsular, the circuit was almost entirely surrounded by sea and was a demanding course. Soon after the start was an S-bend, followed by an acute right-hand corner, then came a short climb with a difficult descent to a right-hand hairpin bend and, finally, there was another bend leading back to the start.

The proceeds from these meetings went to the local hospital (remember this was before the days of the National Health Service). Most races were for up to 10 competitors but, on occasions, as little as three riders. Another feature was team races, for example between riders from the Pendennis and Exeter Clubs.

Pendennis programme from 1937.

Plymouth

Central Park, Plymouth, was the setting for a road race meeting on Bank Holiday Monday 1 August 1938.

Sadly the event was marred by torrential rain and a violent thunderstorm. Only one final and several heats had been completed when the meeting had to be abandoned. It was a great disappointment to the Plymouth Motor Club who had organised the meeting and done much to make the racing possible.

Competitors were enthusiastic about the course that the 200-acre park provided. In all there were 118 entries for the 21-race programme.

St Eval

First used in 1966, the Cornish airfield circuit of St Eval, some four miles (6.5km) from the North Cornish holiday resort of Newquay, was also the first to be used in the county since World War Two. It was a 'competitors-only' event, however, with spectators barred because of security and insurance problems.

Staverton programme from 1972.

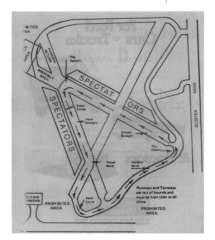

Staverton map from 1975.

Sutton Veney map from 1950.

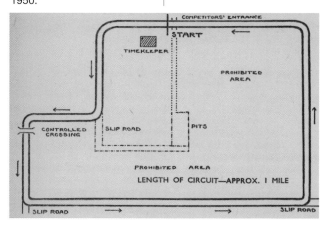

Then in 1967 a second meeting, originally to be held in September that year, was cancelled due to the infamous Torrey Canyon oil tanker disaster, St Eval being a storage depot and distribution centre for the detergent still being used to clean up the beaches polluted by the tanker's oil.

STAVERTON

The Cheltenham Motor Club (founded in 1906) organised meetings at Staverton from the 1969 season into the 1970s. This was a typical airfield circuit, making use of a runway and part of the perimeter track. Running in an anti-clockwise direction, the course measured 1.65 miles (2.65km). During 1972 three meetings were held at the Gloucestershire venue in March, May and September, with the lap record standing at 91.46mph (147.16km/h) set by Dave Pendlebury (Bennett Triumph 3).

SUTTON VENEY

The Wylye Valley Motor Cycle Club first ran meetings at the Imber Road circuit from 1948, but it made a switch to the REME camp at nearby Sutton Veney near Warminster for its meeting of 23 July 1950.

Measuring 1.1 miles (1.8km) in length, this new course was rectangular in shape with a smaller rectangle 'stuck on one end' as a period commentator described it. The surface was mainly concrete, but the finishing straight was a wide tarmac strip reduced in width by straw bales for two-thirds of its length.

Running in an anti-clockwise direction, the course turned left soon after the start and then, after approximately the same distance, turned right, the only right-hander in the lap. Two more short straights, linked by a left-hand bend, brought the rider on to the bottom and longest straight, about a third of a mile (0.52km), and then the Home Straight was reached. The winners of the four main races at this initial meeting were John Hogan 125 (BSA), Cecil Sandford 350cc (Velocette), Geoff Monty Novices (AJS) and J.P.E. Hodgkin Unlimited (Vincent HRD). The fastest lap speeds were just under 50mph (80km/h).

A second meeting was staged on 24 September 1950 and, although the weather was bad, there were still relatively large numbers of spectators. The main race of the day, the Unlimited final, was won by Norton-mounted Les Archer Jnr.

No more racing took place at Sutton Veney due to military requirements.

Thruxton

The first news that Thruxton airfield, near Andover in Hampshire, was to be used for motorcycle racing came when it was announced in February 1950 that the ACU had issued a permit for an Easter Monday open meeting.

The secretary was Neville Goss (who held the post for many, many years), and it was to be organised by the Southampton and District club assisted by the Bishop's Waltham club.

The course, running in a clockwise direction, measured 1.895 miles (3.049km) and included the tarmac perimeter track and runways. Races were to be for 350 and 500cc solos and sidecar classes, and there was also a non-Experts 1000cc event.

This first meeting at the beginning of April 1950 took place in front of what *The Motor Cycle* described as a 'large crowd' who braved gale force winds and rain to watch nearly 100 competitors. The circuit embraced three straights on the runways and some swerves on the perimeter track. In spite of the awful weather conditions the standard of racing was high, with Norton works rider Geoff Duke showing 'invincible' style. Besides Duke being victorious in the 350 and 500cc events, Robin Sherry (348cc AJS) won the 1000cc non-Experts and Jack Surtees (998cc Vincent) the sidecar race. Duke set the fastest lap of the meeting on his 499cc Norton at 72.15mph (116.08km/h).

A much more ambitious programme was put on by the two clubs for their second and final meeting of 1950 at the Hampshire circuit as both 125 and 250cc machines were also catered for. Duke won the 350cc final with Sid Barnett (Norton) the 500cc. John Hogan (BSA) was the 125cc victor and Maurice Cann (Moto Guzzi) took the 250cc laurels. Dave Bennett (Norton) won the non-Experts, with Pip Harris (600cc Norton) winning the sidecar event from Cyril Smith and Jack Surtees having to be content with third spot.

All in all Thruxton seemed a popular venue, certainly when compared to Silverstone, the latter suffering what one period commentator described as more 'airfielditis.'

By the following year, both crowd and entries had swollen to bigger numbers. Circuit newcomers included Cecil Sandford, Bill Doran and several other notable names. The highlight of the year was the ACU International meeting on August Bank

Programme and map from 1951.

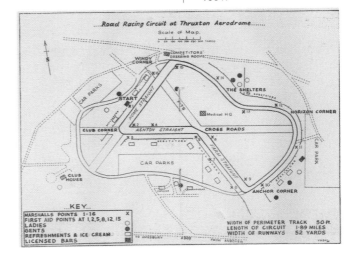

Ray Amm on a 350 Norton,
Thruxton 1951.

Programme, 1952.

Programme, 1956.

Holiday Monday. This included the Festival of Britain invitation race which was broadcast on BBC Radio. Although staged in appalling weather conditions (torrential rain), it was John Surtees who, riding his Vincent Grey Flash single, was the standout performer, chasing double world champion Geoff Duke (works Norton) home in the main event.

Surprisingly, only a few weeks later, in late September 1951, the Ashton Combine put on another international meeting. This time the weather played ball, providing perfect conditions. Les Graham (MV Agusta), making his Thruxton debut, won the 125cc event plus the main race (the latter on his 500cc four-cylinder model). Other winners were Tommy Wood (250cc Moto Guzzi), Dave Bennett (350cc and unlimited Nortons) and Pip Harris (sidecar Norton).

By the mid-1950s Thruxton had become very much the southern racing centre, with, from 1955, the Nine Hours (later rebranded the 500-Miler) Production race, while the big annual ACU meeting became the event at which the British Championship titles were awarded.

Unfortunately, from the early–1960s Thruxton began to suffer from an increasingly poor track surface. Already the British Championships had transferred to Oulton Park, while the final year of the 500-Miler was 1964, and then the venue was lost to racing for several years.

By the beginning of 1968 a new Thruxton circuit had been created, measuring 2.356 miles (3.790km). On 21 April that year the Southampton club ran its first national meeting at the new course.

Geoff Monty riding a 348 Norton, Thruxton, August, 1958, British Championship.

Programme, 1960.

Glorious sunshine lit the face-lifted Wiltshire circuit, and some 10,000 spectators welcomed the newly finished tarmac. Of course, by now there were new names, most notably Dave Croxford (496cc Seeley) who won both the 500 and 1000cc events, where he also established a record lap of 90.81mph (146.11km/h).

The 500-Miler returned in 1969, and the race saw victory for the factory-supported Triumph Bonneville of Percy Tait and Malcolm Uphill. In 1970 the FIM allowed prototypes to compete in the international long-distance

Programme, 1963.

Steve Bateman, Thruxton, summer 1982.

races, and Norton's new Norvil Commando, ridden by Peter Williams and Charlie Sanby, won after the worst rainstorms ever seen in a long-distance event. As someone who took part in that race, I can recall this all too well!

In the present time Thruxton continues as one of the BSB (British Superbike) rounds. It also has the distinction of being the circuit with the highest lap speeds in the series and as such remains a popular venue for both riders and spectators alike.

WESTON-SUPER-MARE

Over 7,000 spectators filled the grandstands along the promenade at Weston-super-Mare in early October 1949 to watch the first (and only) motorcycle road race meeting to be held there (not including, of course, the popular sand races that have been staged on the beach over the years).

To call it 'road racing' required a stretch of the imagination, as the course was the length of the promenade with two tight hairpin turns at each end. The lap measured 1.25 miles (2km). Competitors rode in a clockwise direction, starting on the road and returning along the pavement. The change of surface from road to pavement, from rough to smooth, caused many problems, while the sharp hairpins slowed riders to a crawl, and it became a race from corner to corner – the first man into a bend having the advantage.

Among the 62 entries was an impressive array of riding talent, including Bill Lomas, Bob Foster, Les Archer Jnr and Maurice Cann. It was Lomas who came out on top, winning the 250, 350 and 500cc races.

Dennis Oldham (Yamaha TZ) in winning form at Wroughton, April 1979.

WROUGHTON

At the beginning of the 1970s Wroughton, near Swindon in Wiltshire, measuring 3.4 miles (5.5km), had the distinction at that time of being Britain's longest short circuit (not to be confused with road courses).

Like the other two venues used by the North Gloucestershire MCC, Keevil and Gaydon, Wroughton was an airfield circuit staged in conjunction with the RAFMSA (Royal Air Force Motor Sports Association). These meetings attracted huge entries – varying from 410 to 500 in number.

The 1972 club champions were 125 Chas Ford (Yamaha), 250 Rod Scivyer (Yamaha), 350 Pete Casey (Yamaha), 500 John Goodall (Matchless) and 1000cc Roger Corbett (Dunstall), with sidecars Chris Nickels, passengered by Jim Widdas (Komnik).

WYMERING PARK

Path racing was a feature of the inter-war years. One such venue was the Portsmouth Motor Club's small cinder-surfaced circuit at Wymering Park, Portsmouth. This had two acute bends, and many meetings were staged each year during the early 1930s, with large crowds in attendance.

MIDLANDS

Alton Towers (1953–58)
Ansty (1946–51)
Chirk Castle (1948)
Church Lawford (early 1960s)
Darley Moor (1965–)
Donington Park (1931–37, 1977–)
Gamston (1951)
Gaydon (1970s)
Haddenham (1949)
Hanley Park (1934)
Long Marston (late 1970s–early 1980s)
Mallory Park (1956–)
Osmaston Manor (1952–57)
Park Hall (1928–39)
Perton (Mid 1960s)
Prees Heath (Early 1960s)
Retford Project (1949)
Rockingham Castle (1946)
Rockingham (2001–)
Silverstone (1949–)
Syston (1929–mid 1930s)
Wellesbourne (late 1960s–late 1970s)

ALTON TOWERS

Now world famous as a major tourist attraction, Alton Towers, located between Uttoxeter and Ashbourne in Staffordshire, had an earlier life in the 1950s as a motorcycle racing circuit.

Its life as a circuit began at the end of March 1953 when the course, measuring 0.85 miles (1.36km), was lapped by a quartet of well-known East Midland Centre riders under poor weather conditions, at just under 60mph (96.5km/h). Previously the scene of the 1952 ACU National Rally, the racing lap included two fast bends, one hairpin and two approximately 90-degree corners all running to the right.

The first meeting took place on 5 July 1953, but it was the second meeting held at the end of September that year which was more notable, as considerable improvements had been made by then, especially in the fencing

Alton Towers programme from 1953.

around the track. As was perhaps to be expected, many of the riders who competed at nearby Osmaston Manor course also took in Alton Towers, including Peter Ferbrache, Johnny Eckert and Fred Wallis.

Into 1954, and it was Peter Ferbrache who dominated the April meeting on his 350 and 500cc Hartley Ariels before what *The Motor Cycle* described as a 'large crowd'. There were two other meetings that season at the venue in late August and at the end of September. At the first of these, Ferbrache once again dominated the proceedings, but the final one saw George Catlin and Johnny Eckert both win a race.

In the first meeting of the season at Alton Towers in April 1955 Cecil Sandford won the 350cc race on a ex-works Moto Guzzi and finished runner-up to Johnny Eckert (Excelsior) in the 250cc race (also riding a Guzzi). In the three bigger races (500cc, Unlimited and Invitation) honours were shared by John Hodgkin, J. Denton and Peter Ferbrache.

The second meeting of 1955 saw the Pathfinders and Derby Club win the East Midlands Centre Championship over the Nottingham Tornados. The third and final event of 1955 saw Peter Ferbrache gain new 350 and 500cc race record speeds of 51.65mph (83.10km/h) and 52.63mph (84.68km/h) respectively.

In late April 1956 newcomer Terry Shepherd of Liverpool (later to become a works rider for MV Agusta) made a winning debut at Alton Towers on a Norton in the 350cc race, while Howard Grindley (200cc), Brian Purslow (250cc) and Peter Ferbrache (1000cc) all won at record speeds.

Alton Towers circuit map from 1953.

Alton Towers in 1955, showing the tree-lined nature of the Staffordshire circuit.

Alf Briggs in winning form on his 500cc JAP-engined Triumph special. The JAP engine proved ideal for the tight, twisty nature of the Alton Towers course.

The following month the Leicester Query club won the East Midlands Centre Championship, while Terry Shepherd was victorious in the 250cc event in the year's final meeting at the end of September.

In 1957 there were again three meetings in March, April and September. This year saw the arrival of Peter Middleton to challenge the likes of Ferbrache, Wallis and Eckert. It also saw a young John Cooper from Derby first make his mark gaining leaderboard position in the 200cc class on a Lomas-Triumph.

The March 1958 meeting saw a heat victory in the 350cc class for Phil Read, but once again it was Peter Ferbrache who won the main 1000cc final (now riding a Norton). Sadly this was to be the final motorcycle race meeting at Alton Towers. For many Midland enthusiasts its loss, together with Osmaston Manor, was only partly offset by the opening of Mallory Park, near Leicester, as both Alton Towers and Osmaston Manor brought a unique Parklands type arena to the Midlands racing scene.

ANSTY

Ansty, near Coventry, was yet another airfield that became a popular venue during the immediate post-World War Two era. Organised by the Antelope MCC, itself a comparatively new club formed as a development from the wartime Home Guard motorcycle activities in 1944, its first meeting was staged at the beginning of November 1946 and was something of a gamble as the weather could well have been a problem. But as *The Motor Cycle* dated 7 November 1946 reveals 'the meeting was a noteworthy success', with

1948 programme cover.

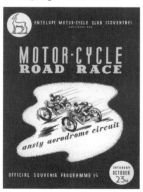

some 140 entries and spectators in many thousands. As one report stated 'the circuit was one of the best, if not the best, yet found on an airfield.'

The circuit, measuring 1.75 miles (2.81km) in length, was roughly D-shaped with the main straight almost three-quarters of a mile and the start line about halfway. At the end was a slow, almost-hairpin turn to the right, then a right-angle left bend, followed by four easy right-hand curves and a right-angle corner exiting into the straight. As with the majority of other airfield circuits the width of the roads permitted riders to pass comfortably, while the surface, part-concrete and part-tarmac, providing surprisingly good grip even when damp. The course ran in a clockwise direction.

Among riders at this first meeting were competitors from France and Belgium. With men such as Harold Daniell, Fergus Anderson, George Brown, Bob Foster, Sid Barnett and Peter Goodman, plus sidecar stars including Eric Oliver and Jackie Beeton, the racing was fast and furious. Daniell (Norton) took the 350 and 500cc finals, Fergus Anderson (Moto Guzzi) the 250cc and Eric Oliver the sidecar event.

As the world's leading rider of his day it is worth noting that Geoff Duke rode at Ansty for the first time in October 1948 and for the last, two years later, on 7 October 1950. On the latter occasion, riding works Featherbed Nortons, he

1951 Ansty course map.

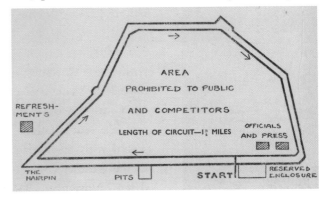

won five races and set a new course lap record of 87.74mph (141.17km/h). The previous record had been set by George Brown riding a 998cc Vincent HRD at 81.84mph (131.68km/h) on 25 June 1949. And, of course, Duke's five-hundred Norton had an engine size half that of Brown's machine.

Other Ansty top men of the early 1950s included Dickie Dale, Sid Barnett and Cecil Sandford in the larger solo classes, while Sandford, Bill Lomas and local man Len Bayliss were tops in the 250cc category. Bill Boddice had by now joined Oliver and Beeton as the sidecar kings of Ansty.

Chirk Castle

Although it had not been possible to recreate the popular pre-war circuit races at Park Hall, Oswestry, the local Oswestry Club managed to find a new venue for the 1948 season at Chirk Castle between Oswestry and Llangollen. The first and only event was run on 31 July that year.

Church Lawford

Church Lawford, some two miles (3.2km) west of Rugby, Warwickshire, was the setting during the 1963 season for several Racing 50 club events.

Darley Moor

Located between Uttoxeter and Ashbourne in Derbyshire, Darley Moor's first application to stage racing events was made in June 1964. The owner of the former airfield, Uttoxeter businessman J. Shemilt, gave a five-year lease to the West Midlands Racing 50 Club who planned to set up a one-and-a-half-mile (2.41km) long course.

When the first meeting took place on Easter Friday, 18 April 1965, however, it was organised by the Darley Moor Motor Cycle Racing Club. Bitter winds swept the Derbyshire airfield, but even so 3,000 hardy fans lined the perimeter for an action-packed day which began at noon but did not finish until 7.30pm. The race winners were as follows: 50cc Mick Pomfret (Honda), 125cc Steve Murray (Honda), 250cc Bill Smith (DMW), 350cc Alan Dugdale (Honda), 500cc Keith Heckles (Norton), production Brian Nadin (Triumph) and sidecar T. Davies (Triumph).

It was Heckles who became the first to win a Darley Moor race at over 70mph (112.63km/h) when he averaged 70.1mph (112.6km/h) at the second meeting on Saturday 16 May 1965 on his 499cc Norton.

Another milestone in the circuit's history came on Whit Monday, 3 June 1968, when Darley held its first races for vintage bikes together with its usual solo and sidecar classes. Also of interest was that at that time the clerk of the course was Hector Dugdale and the commentator was Chris Carter,

Map and programme from 1968.

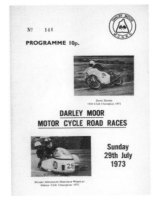

DMW-mounted Peter Humber (36) leads R.J. Minshull on a similar machine at Darley Moor's Hairpin, Easter Monday, 1966.

Programme from 1973.

while there was a record entry of over 330 competitors. Entries for vintage events included Willie Wilshire, Chris Williams and Ivan Rhodes.

Another stalwart of the Darley Moor scene has been ACU official Don Ryder, who has been involved with the Derbyshire venue since the earliest days. For over 40 years, Darley has hosted a vast number of club meetings usually staged on Bank Holiday weekends, which has ensured large numbers of spectators. Although no longer held for several years, Darley also hosted its annual Stars of Darley national meeting. It is also the home of the Mick Boddice Race School.

A unique and excellent feature of Darley Moor circuit is that a perimeter track runs around the majority of the course, allowing broken-down machines to be collected more easily than would otherwise be the case.

DONINGTON PARK

Before World War Two, with the exception of Brooklands, the Ulster Grand Prix and the Isle of Man TT, Donington Park was the most important motorcycle racing circuit in the British Isles. Although Donington was just as important, if not more so, for cars, it was a motorcycle that can claim the honour of being the first motor vehicle to win a race at the Derbyshire venue. This was a 350cc Raleigh ridden by C.F. 'Squib' Burton, who took the honours in the very first-ever meeting at Donington on Whit Monday 1931. Some 20,000 spectators witnessed this historic victory. Amazingly Burton, though a renowned dirt-track racer, was not considered to be a serious

Programme cover from the first race meet at Donington, May 1931.

The Melbourne loop section during the late 1930s.

contender for the race. This first meeting was a roughly laid out affair on the estate of Donington Hall, and the meeting was organised by the local Derby and District Motor Club. The secretary of this club was a certain F.G. (Fred) Craner, himself a notable former TT rider. Craner was to be instrumental throughout the 1930s in making Donington into a major sporting venue, and today his memory is kept alive by the Craner Curves section of the modern circuit. Another little known facet of early Donington history was that German officers were interred there during World War One.

By the beginning of 1932 the circuit had been officially laid out. Measuring a shade over two miles (3.2km) in length, it ran in a clockwise direction. The start and finish led into Hairpin Bend, Thompson's Lane, Starkey's Hill, Starkey's Corner, Redgate Lodge, Holly Wood and from there back to the finish of the lap. The lap was of an irregular shape and included three acute bends and half a dozen faster ones.

Also, by the opening meeting of the 1932 season at Easter much of the course had been remade from the previous year and tarred, while facilities for spectators had been greatly improved. A point of interest was that the profits of this meeting went towards the club's endowment of a bed at the Derbyshire Royal Infirmary. Other Donington meetings, also in aid of the Infirmary, took place at Whitsun and August Bank Holidays.

1939 circuit plan.

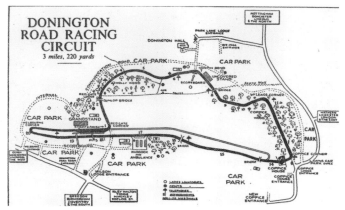

For the remainder of the 1930s Donington Park grew into a major motor sport venue. This was helped by alterations undertaken during the closed season of 1933–34, which saw the track extended to 2.6 miles (2.18km), and again during the winter of 1937–38 when the circuit length was increased again to 3.1 miles (4.9km). This latter alteration saw the introduction of the Melbourne corner section.

June 1933, advertisement for second meeting of the season.

On Saturday 27 August 1938 Donington Park hosted the Dunlop Jubilee International Motor Cycle Races to mark the 50th anniversary of J.B. Dunlop's invention of the Pneumatic Tyre. Just about everyone who was anyone on the British racing scene was there, the entry list including Stanley Woods, Harold Daniell, Freddie Frith, J.H. (Crasher) White, Ted Mellors, Walter Handley, Bob Foster, Jock West and many, many more.

Donington even hosted the speed tests for the International Six Days Trial in both 1937 and 1938. The final meeting at the circuit on the very eve of the outbreak of war came on Saturday 26 August 1939 with the International Grand Prix meeting. At that time the outright motorcycle lap record stood at 77.48mph (124.66km/h) set by Norton works rider Harold Daniell on his 499cc machine.

During the war years Donington played host to the military authorities. Post-war it became what Fred Carter was to describe as 'a dump of various war surplus vehicles' – there being around 80,000 in 1946 at the site!

In late 1966 *Motor Cycle News* published a news story saying 'Donington Park racing circuit is to live on – this now seems pretty certain, with an

1939 programme.

Donington Park Clubman Day, 6 May 1939, at Holly Wood in the 25-mile 250cc race. The front two riders are 45 L.J. Archer (New Imperial) and 8 T. Colllier (CTS).

1978 programme.

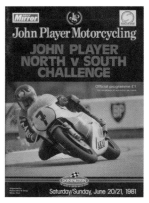

Programme from 1981.

Italian Franco Uncini 500
World Champion (Suzuki) at
Donington in 1982.

Dutchman Boet Van Dulman
(6) and Pete Wild (42),
both on 500 Suzukis,
battle it out at Donington
on 19 June 1982.

enthusiastic owner [A.P. Shields], backing from Grovewood Securities [then owners of the Brands Hatch Group] and great interest from motorcycle and car enthusiasts for its reopening.' This news proved premature, however, and in reality it was not until the rose magnet Tom Wheatcroft purchased the circuit in the early 1970s that Donington was reborn. Major rebuilding work took place including, controversially, removing many historic trees, and the circuit was finally re-opened for motorcycles in 1977.

If the 1970s saw the rebirth of the track, then the 1980s saw the arrival of the British Grand Prix in place of Silverstone and the very first round of the World Superbike Championship in May 1988 (I was there). And although in the 1990s the WSB circus also ran rounds at Brands Hatch (a situation that has continued into the 21st century) the Moto GP series (which has replaced the old Grand Prix system) remains at Donington for the British round.

As for the circuit itself, the lap begins with a sprint into the right-hand Redgate Corner and thereafter the fast downhill sweep through Craner Curves to the Old Hairpin. Then comes the climb uphill to McLean's and the short straight to Coppice and the high-speed section back to the paddock. In 1985 a new section of the track was constructed behind the paddock, replicating the famous pre-war Melbourne Hairpin.

Donington Park, Gold Cup
start, summer 1983.
Number 7 is Barry Sheene
(Suzuki).

Donington also houses one of the biggest and best-known motorcycle/car racing museums in the world. And no one can dispute that considerable investment has been made from the mid-1970s onwards; however, to the author's mind, Donington (together with the modern Silverstone) has become cold – too professional is maybe the best description – and in the process has lost the magic which is still there in circuits such as Cadwell Park, Brands Hatch and most certainly road courses such as Scarborough. Other modern-day Donington attractions are the ongoing Sunday Market and pop concerts, to name but two.

Barry Sheene with his
Suzuki RG500 at Donington
in 1984. This was one of
Barry's last races as he
retired at the end of the
year.

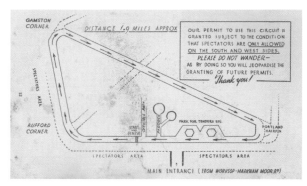

Map and programme from Gamston airfield.

GAMSTON

Gamston airfield, Nottinghamshire, was the setting for a road race meeting organised by the Sheffield and Hallamshire Motor Club on 14 July 1951. The circuit, running in a clockwise direction, measured 1.9 miles (3km). The restrictions for this meeting meant that spectators were only allowed on the south and west sides of the venue. There were only three corners, Rufford (a right after the start), Gamston (at the beginning of the longest straight) and finally Portland Hairpin (which led out onto the start and finish line).

There were a total of 129 entries, including eight sidecars, and among these were Denis Parkinson, Len Bayliss, Pip Harris, Bernard Hargreaves, Bill Boddice, Fron Purslow and Eric Housley. There was a total prize fund of £156.

GAYDON

Gaydon was one of three circuits used by the North Gloucestershire MCC in partnership with the Royal Air Force Motor Sports Association during the 1970s (the others being Keevil in Wiltshire and Wroughton near Swindon).

At that time Gaydon was a former operational V-bomber base, which in the early 1970s was used as a clearing station for Africans who had arrived in Britain from Amin's Uganda.

In 1972 the clerk of the course, Brian Chapman, explained the regular routine for race meetings at Gaydon, saying, 'We arrive at the circuit at 4pm

Gaydon was yet another airfield circuit, thanks to the RAF's enthusiasm for motorcycle racing.

on Friday and work until dark. Then we sleep on camp beds in an RAF building. We work from 6am until dark again on Saturday, putting up 2,500 stakes, three miles [4.8km] of rope and placing 200 marker cones and 350 straw bales. We like to have the course finished the day before the racing. Sunday's racing usually finished just before 6 o'clock and we have everything cleared away before 9.30pm.'

1973 programme and circuit plan.

The Gaydon circuit was one and a half miles (2.4km) and ran in a clockwise direction. In 1973 there were four meetings at Gaydon, in April, May, June and September.

HADDENHAM

To replace Dunholme the BMCRC opened its new Haddenham circuit on Sunday 27 March 1949. Among the entry list were Les Graham, Bill Doran, Geoff Duke, Maurice Cann and George Brown.

Haddenham was situated between Aylesbury and Thame in Buckinghamshire, some 45 miles (72km) from London and 55 miles (88.5km) from the industrial Midlands.

This first meeting saw George Brown (499cc Vincent HRD) dominate. He won two of three 351–1000cc races and also won the 350–1000cc.

As for the circuit, this was 2.2 miles (3.5km) in length and included two

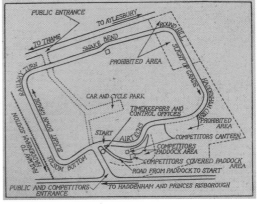

Programme and plan for 1949.

straights and another with a slight loop. The lower side of the course had a slow S-bend, and there were four right-hand bends. The surface was concrete with a thin, patchy coating of tar. A large disadvantage of Haddenham for major events was the narrowness of the track.

The second meeting held in mid-May saw Sid Barnett challenging George Brown for the main honours, with Dickie Dale coming out on top of the three-fifties.

Haddenham airfield, near Aylesbury in Buckinghamshire, was used for racing by Bemsee after Dunholme and before Silverstone, 1949.

The third meeting in early June was billed as 'Non-Star', the most interesting feature being separate 'one-make' 350cc races for AJS, Norton and Velocette machines respectively.

The fourth and final meeting at Haddenham took place on Saturday 2 July 1949. Again George Brown (Vincents) proved the master in the 500cc and Unlimited event, and the same rider also equalled his existing lap record of 74.59mph (120km/h) on his 998cc 'Gunga Din' model.

But, with Silverstone coming on stream for future BMCRC events, Haddenham was quietly forgotten. This meant that 1949 was to be the only year that Haddenham witnessed motorcycle racing, which might seem a pity but in truth Silverstone was so much more superior that one can quite understand the decision.

HANLEY PARK

On Saturday 28 July 1934 the Hanley Park Horticultural Show gave the local Stoke-on-Trent MCC a chance to run a race meeting there. The event was held over a 0.5-mile (0.8km) circuit, although 'circuit' is hardly the word suitable to describe the semi-circular asphalt path around the park. There were three events. The first restricted to members of north Staffordshire clubs, a 350cc Experts and a 500cc Experts. The 350cc race was won by Les Kitchen of Liverpool who was the fastest with an average speed of 40.03mph (64.4km/h), this giving an accurate portrayal of the tightness of the course.

LONG MARSTON

Long Marston, between Stratford upon Avon and Evesham in Warwickshire, saw races run by the Cheltenham Motor Club during the late

1970s and early 1980s. For example, in 1982 there were three meetings in March, May and August.

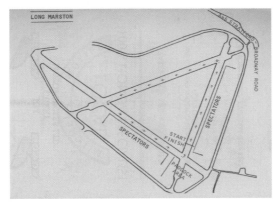

Long Marston programme and map.

The meeting held there on Sunday 16 May 1982 saw no fewer than 24 races. As a general rule there were four laps for heats and six for the finals and included a round of the 50cc UK Championships, the leading riders in the 'tiddler' class being Steve Patrickson (Kreidler), Ian McConnachie (ASPS) and Ron Ponti (Kreidler). Other riders of note that day included veteran Welshman Ken Finney (125cc Honda and 250cc Ducati). As for lap speeds up to that time, the course record stood at 85.37mph (137.36km/h) achieved by Suzuki-mounted M. Preston.

The track, approximately one mile (1.61km) in length, ran in an anti-clockwise direction and was triangular in shape.

MALLORY PARK

Mallory Park history goes back many centuries and was for many years a country estate, the Mallory family being direct ancestors of the late Queen Mother, Lady Elizabeth Bowes-Lyon and consequently the reigning British Royal Family.

Immediately after World War Two, a 1,660-yard oval grass track was completed, not for motor sport but horses! But this venture got into financial difficulties. After this, the Leicester Query Club then rented the track to put on motorcycle grass track races between 1949 and 1954.

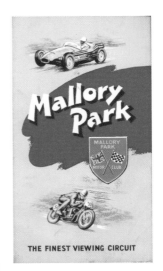

Map and programme from 1958.

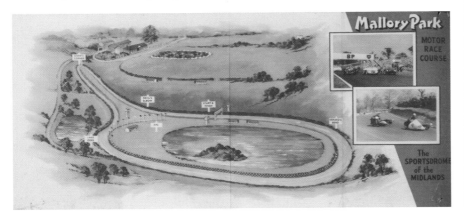

The 18th-century hall was occupied by the British army during the war but was demolished in 1952, although the coach house and stable block were left standing. The buildings eventually became the circuit offices, workshops and the Coach House Hotel, pub and restaurant.

In 1953 the entire estate was purchased at auction by H.W. Moult of Derby, but in 1955 it was taken over by Clive Wormleighton from Earl Shilton. Clive was a motor sport enthusiast and can rightly be described as the father of the Mallory Park race circuit.

Clive Wormleighton utilised the existing oval of the grass track and added the Hairpin, thus providing a circuit of 1.35 miles (2.17km). A key feature of Mallory has always been its compact nature, providing a close view of the racing.

The official opening of the new tarmac circuit occurred on Wednesday 26 April 1956. The ceremony included some laps by Bob Gerard (Cooper Bristol car) and Maurice Cann (250 Moto Guzzi). Gerard's Bend (the long ,sweeping corner that comprises almost a quarter of the circuit's length) was named in recognition of the assistance Bob Gerard had given Clive Wormleighton in the circuit's completion.

The inaugural motorcycle race meeting took place on 13 May 1956, and with vast crowds in attendance the very first race was started by Maurice Cann. From the start (Kirby Straight) riders negotiated Gerard's Bend, followed by Stebbe Straight, the Lake Esses, the hairpin (Shaw's Corner), followed by the Devil's Elbow and finally back to the start and finish line.

Nottingham Tornado Motor Club road races at Mallory Park, 14 April 1957, led by John Patrick (250cc Velocette) approaching the hairpin.

On 30 September 1962 the ownership of Mallory Park passed to Grovewood Securities, a London-based property and investment company, which later the same year also acquired Brands Hatch, followed by Snetterton and Oulton Park. Later still, in 1983 the circuit was purchased by Leeds businessman, car racer and enthusiast Chris Meek. Finally, in January 2005 the circuit was acquired by BARC (British Automobile Racing Club), who had owned Thruxton since the late 1960s and Pembrey from the early 1990s. A special mention should be made of the Overend family, who organised meetings during Chris Meek's ownership (in other words from 1963 through to 2004 inclusive).

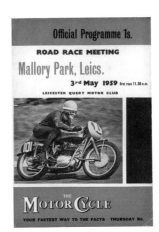

Programme from 1959.

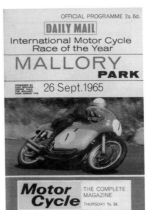

Programme from 1965.

Programme from 1971.

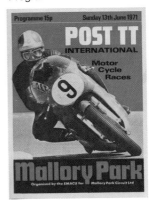

Giacomo Agostini after winning the Race of the Year at Mallory in September 1967.

Riders sweeping down from Devil's Elbow, down Kirby Straight and into Gerard's Bend; 1999.

A Suzuki Katana leading a production race at the hairpin, Mallory Park, 1981.

Mallory Park 2007 events
programme.

Osmaston Manor
programme, 1952.

Probably the glory days of Mallory Park were the 1960s and 1970s.
During those years virtually every star rider, British and foreign, raced at
Mallory – men such as Mike Hailwood, Giacomo Agostini, Barry Sheene,
Kenny Roberts. You could name them and they had been to the relatively
small Leicestershire track. And even though it still hosts a round of the
British Superbike Championship, changes made to slow machines have, in
the author's opinion, dampened down both rider and spectator interest.

OSMASTON MANOR

Osmaston Manor was part of a private park that was the
property of the Lord Lieutenant of Derbyshire, Sir Ian Walker.
The circuit measured 0.75 miles (1.2km), and as one period
report commented, 'writhes through a classic example of an
English country house estate.' The surface was tarmac, and the
lap was of varying widths, with both right and left-hand bends
slightly undulating . In one section the track was so sinuous (and
narrow) that overtaking was prohibited.

At the first meeting organised, as were subsequent events, by the
Pathfinders and Derby Club, it was soon discovered that the circuit
was ideally suited to engines with straight-through rather than
megaphone exhausts, acceleration being much more important
than all-out top end performance. There were classes for 200,
250, 350 and 500cc solos, with the main event the 20-lap
250–1000cc Derby Cup being won by Peter Davey (Triumph) at
an average speed of 53.09mph (86.72km/h). Other winners were
200cc V. Parker (riding Bill Lomas's 197cc James), 250cc Peter

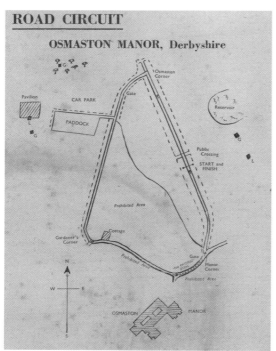

ROAD CIRCUIT

OSMASTON MANOR, Derbyshire

Osmaston Manor circuit plan from 1952.

Doncaster (BSA), 350cc Fred Wallis (AJS), and 500cc Peter Davey taking his second victory on his Triumph twin.

In 1952 two meetings were staged, one in mid-July the other at the end of August. A notable entry was Molly Briggs (the well known trials rider) who rode a DOT into second place in the 200cc event while Peter Davey set a new race record of 54.39mph (87.51km/h) on his five-hundred Triumph. In the second of the 1952 meetings the bigger classes saw a battle royal between Davey, John Hodgkin (Vincent HRD), Fred Wallis (AJS) and Peter Ferbrache (Hartley Ariel), and it was Wallis who emerged victorious in the Derby Cup race.

In May 1953 new lap records were established in the 200, 250 and 500cc classes by Howard Grindley (148cc Royal Enfield) and Peter Ferbrache (249 and 497cc Ariels). In the main race of the day Peter Davey (Triumph) won after Ferbrache crashed.

A year later in May 1954, Ferbrache made amends by winning the Wingfield Cup at a record average speed of 54.93mph (88.38km/h). In the now traditional manner, the second meeting later that year, at the end of August, also saw Ferbrache take the main Derby Cup race but at a much slower speed due to torrential rain.

With Ferbrache away in the Isle of Man, John Hodgkin (Vincent HRD) won the main race in late May 1955, the only meeting at the circuit that year.

The next meeting was on August Bank Holiday Monday 1956 when Peter Ferbrache returned to win the 350, 500 and 1000cc races. Other winners that day were 200cc Pete Tomes (Royal Enfield) and 250cc Fron Purslow (NSU).

Unfortunately, the Whitsun meeting in June 1957 was to be the last to be held at the picturesque Derbyshire venue. This was due to the landowner fitting cattle grids to the road. And so yet another popular racing circuit was lost to the public. The race winners on that final day were 200cc Alf Briggs (husband of Molly) riding a Triumph Cub, 250cc Pete Tomes (JAP), 350cc Alf Briggs (Triumph), 500cc Pete Minion (Norton) and the Derby Cup (251–1000cc) Fred Wallis (348cc BSA).

PARK HALL

The Oswestry and District Motor Club organised a series of race meetings over the local Park Hall, Oswestry, circuit from the late 1920s until the very eve of World War Two.

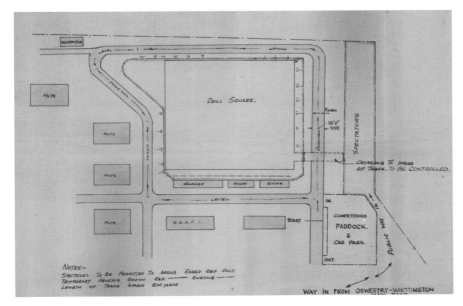

Park Hall course map.

The course measured some 0.6 miles (1km) in length. Due to the tightness of the track and the sharp nature of several corners, lap speeds were what would now be regarded as exceedingly slow. For example, at the Easter Friday meeting in March 1932 R.L. Graham (499cc Rudge) set a new record speed of 37.2mph (59.9km/h).

It was traditional at Park Hall to stage the meetings on public holidays, other examples being Whitsun Monday and the summer August break, and also to have team competitions.

Park Hall continued throughout the remainder of the 1930s, but then in spring 1939 came the surprise news that the venue had been sold for army purposes and, although the Whit Monday meeting would not be affected, it was 'unlikely' that further racing would be held on the existing course for some time.

When the first meeting was staged back in 1928 it had been over another section of the estate, and the club said it hoped to use this in the future. Unfortunately, all this came to no avail due to the outbreak of war in September.

So at the end of May 1939 came the final meeting at the by-now famous track – even then there were signs of military occupation. As for the racing itself, the weather was 'glorious' (*The Motor Cycle*), while riders included Tommy Wood (Velocette). The last race was a 10-mile (16km) 600cc race which was won by Jack Wilkinson (OK Supreme).

And so Park Hall ended, and the final announcement over the loudspeakers said, 'Not farewell, but we'll be seeing you somewhere and somewhen soon.' But the war changed all that, and racing never returned.

1932 programme.

1964 Perton programme.

1961 programme and map.

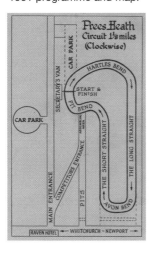

PERTON

Perton, Tettenhall, on the western fringes of Wolverhampton in the West Midlands, was the home of the Birmingham-based Midland Motor Cycle Racing Club during the mid-1960s and was to be the scene of several meetings over the years. In its first year, 1964, there were three dates: 25 April, 4 July and 5 September.

For their very first meeting on 25 April 1964 there were a total of 149 solos and 29 sidecars. Notable entries included Tony Rutter (348cc Norton), John Rudge (348cc Norton), Trevor Burgess (50cc Itom, 125cc Honda), Keith Heckles (348cc Norton), Steve Jolly (348cc Norton), Ron Pladdys (124cc Honda, 246cc Aermacchi), P.J. Walsh (125cc MV Agusta, 250cc Ariel) and Barry Davis (200cc Ducati).

There were 27 races with an amazing number of different makes of machinery, including such rarities as a 125cc Montesa, 125cc Rumi, 350cc RCA and a large number of specials.

The 1.27-mile (2.04km) circuit usually hosted five-lap races, thus enabling the very maximum number of races in a single day to take place.

PREES HEATH

Prees Heath circuit near Whitchurch in Shropshire, was a popular venue for club events during the early 1960s. The circuit, very similar to the shorter Brands Hatch course of the early 1950s, measured 1.15 miles (1.85km) and ran in a clockwise direction. The start–finish line lay directly before the long sweeping Hartles Bend, then came The Long Straight (correctly named!), the hairpin-like Avon Bend, The Short Straight, followed by the only left on the circuit which led directly into Pit Bend and the finish line.

Although Prees Heath was a 'club' circuit, it nonetheless seemed to attract several well-known riders, certainly in the early days. For example the meeting run on Sunday 20 August 1961 saw the entry include the likes of Fron Purslow (125cc Ducati, 250cc Honda and BSA Sidecar), Bill Smith (350cc AJS7R), Alan Dugdale (125cc Ducati, 250cc NSU Sportmax and a Production ride), Steve Murray (125cc Honda, 350cc AJS, 500cc Matchless G50), Derek Woodman (348cc, 499cc Nortons and a Production ride) and Keith Heckles (348cc BSA Gold Star). However it was a young Stuart Graham who got all of the publicity for his rides in the 125 and 250cc events.

Another feature of Prees Heath meetings was the inclusion of a Production machine race.

RETFORD PROJECT

In the summer of 1949 it was revealed that there was an ambitious scheme to build a road racing circuit in conjunction with the Mansfield and District Motor Cycle Club. The site was the Grove Hall estate, some one and a half miles (2.41km) from Retford and the Great North Road (A1). The park was of 150 acres and the proposal was to construct a two-mile (3.21km) circuit with a tarmac surface. A feature of the course was a steep climb about 0.5 miles (0.8km) up the coach road to the hall.

It was stated that the scheme was backed by the Retford Borough Council and the Retford Rural Council and had been approved by the Town and County Planning Authority; however, nothing was to come of this interesting project.

ROCKINGHAM

Rockingham Motor Speedway near Corby, Northamptonshire, was mainly constructed in an attempt to bring American Indy Car racing to Britain. It was built in 2000 and opened the following year. Essentially there were three circuits – an outer 'Speedway' with banked curves, and an inner 'Kart-like' track, plus a combination of the two; however, in an attempt to attract top-class motorcycle events to the complex, the circuit owners joined the two circuits to make one that could host a round of the British Superbike (BSB) series. This did not prove popular with riders due to the closeness of the walls on the outside of the banked sections of the course. Although subsequent changes were made. Rockingham has not become a permanent venue for BSB, nor has it really proved popular for other motorcycle meetings.

The author was there in his role as coach for the ACU Academy in the summer of 2001, and it is his opinion that the National inner circuit proved ideal for 125cc machines.

In 2008, when this book was being compiled, Rockingham listed a wide range of activities, including corporate events, track days and, of course, car racing.

The lengths of the three circuits are as follows: the International 2.54 miles (4.08km), Oval 1.5-miles (2.41km)and National 1.7-miles (2.73km).

ROCKINGHAM CASTLE

Rockingham Castle staged a single meeting in June 1946 and is not to be confused with the modern Rockingham, although both venues are near each other, with Corby, Northamptonshire, as their local town.

This 1946 event was organised by the combined efforts of Irthlingborough 'Bats' MCC and the Stewarts & Lloyds MCC. The circuit was 840 yards in

1946 programme.

length and roughly oblong in shape. The surface was loose in places and extremely narrow, so narrow in fact that only two riders could be on the circuit at one time and only 14 competitors took part in the meeting!

This did not prevent an unfortunate accident, however, when, as *The Motor Cycle* described, the riderless machine continued 'for about 50 yards before it plunged against the rope that held back the crowd. Regrettably, one woman was injured.' This incident and the narrowness of the course were probably the reasons why this was the one and only meeting at Rockingham Castle.

Silverstone

In the summer of 1948 it was announced that, after many months of negotiation with the Air Ministry, the RAC (Royal Automobile Club) had obtained a lease to use the now redundant wartime airfield at Silverstone near Towcester, Northamptonshire. This was also the very first time that the RAC had taken the full financial responsibility for running a race circuit. At that time *The Motor Cycle* was able to report in its 8 July 1948 issue, 'As it is at present, the surface is good. The course resembles a figure of eight and is four miles [6.4km] in length.' Actually, the precise lap distance was 3.7 miles (5.95km), and Jimmy Brown was appointed the first track manager.

When the first meeting (cars) took place in October 1948, it was a very basic affair, with makeshift pits put up at the farm, while hay bales marked out the course. As one commentator so aptly described the scene, 'The dominant feature of Silverstone is the immense canopy of the sky, clouds ponderously scudding by often laden with rain.' That first meeting attracted around 120,000 people, many of whom did not pay to get in! It was obvious right from the start that Silverstone was just in the right location, equally accessible from the north, south, east and west.

Early 1949 brought news that the RAC was to make Silverstone available for two wheels as well as four. As the RAC were in charge of car meetings at Silverstone this role was taken on by the BMCRC for motorcycles. Notably, a condition which the RAC (and thus the BMCRC) accepted was that racing at Silverstone meant that the various other airfields controlled by the Air Ministry or other government departments should no longer be used for racing. This was to cause a lot of discontent among other clubs as the Silverstone charges (made by the RAC) were such that they were too high a figure to allow its use by anyone other than the BMCRC.

The first and only motorcycle meeting to be staged at the Northamptonshire venue in 1949 was held on Saturday 8 October and was no less an occasion than the annual Hutchinson 100 (which for the previous two seasons had been held at Dunholme and pre-war Brooklands).

1950 programme.

Winners of the principal events were Maurice Cann (250cc Moto Guzzi), Peter Romaine (350cc AJS) and Les Graham (500cc AJS). Graham put up the fastest lap at 90.05mph (145km/h). The lap distance for this first motorcycle event was given at just under three miles (4.82km).

When the next bike meeting was run, *Motor Cycling's* Silverstone Saturday 22 April 1950, the circuit was essentially the one used the year before except for improvements made to the surface and how it was marked (using small, white plastic markers). Running in a clockwise direction. the first corner was Woodcote, followed by Copse, Maggotts Curve, Becketts, Chapel Curve, Hanger Straight, Stowe, Club, Abbey Curve and so back to the start–finish.

At that April 1950 meeting Cann again emerged victorious in the 250 and Graham in the first 350cc event. In the second 350cc and the 400–1000cc event Geoff Duke (Nortons) came out on top, but the lap record was not broken.

The 1950s had also seen several changes at Silverstone, notable in 1951 the RAC had given up the lease, handing the track over to the BRDC (British Racing Drivers' Club). The pits were moved from the farm to the straight between Woodcote and Copse corners, thus introducing a club circuit leaving the Grand Prix course just before Becketts and utilising the central runway down to Woodcote.

For the remainder of the decade Silverstone held two major motorcycle meetings each year, the spring *Motor Cycling* Saturday event and the Hutchinson 100 later in the year. But with the arrival of the 1960s the former meeting was axed from the calendar. Even so, Silverstone remained an important circuit for motorcycle events, though cars were its main

1951 programme and map.

BMCRC Golden Jubilee meeting, Silverstone, 18 April 1959, Bob McIntyre (77) leads from Alastair King (79), Bob Anderson (73) and Mike Hailwood (67).

1954 Hutchinson 100 programme.

1963 map showing start–finish between Woodcote and Copse Corner.

Silverstone, International Hutchinson 100 meeting, April 1962. Riders as follows: 27 Horace Crowder (Bianchi), 39 Arthur Wheeler (Guzzi), 34 Percy Tait (Aermacchi), 42 Mike Hailwood (Benelli), 44 Tommy Robb (Aermacchi), 43 Jim Redman (Honda), 12 Mick Manley (Ducati).

purpose. During 1961, 1962 and 1963 Silverstone hosted a 1,000km (621.4-mile) endurance race for series production machines.

In May 1960 Derek Minter had lapped the Silverstone GP circuit at 100.93mph (162.39km/h) in practice, the first over the 'ton' lap by a motorcyclist at the venue. These were the times when all the top stars raced there, including Minter, Bob McIntyre, Mike Hailwood, Phil Read and John

BMCRC 500cc, Silverstone, 6 April 1963; showing hanger straight, riders are as follows: 4 Phil Read, 7 Joe Dunphy, 1 Derek Minter, 42 John Cooper, 11 Paddy Driver, 2 John Hartle.

Hartle to name just a few. The same applied for the sidecars too. The *Daily Express* newspaper was involved with the BMCRC with its international status Silverstone motorcycle meeting of the 1960s, and into the 1970s when the ACU took over from BMCRC. At the same time the cigarette industry began to be involved in motor sport sponsorship at the top level including motorcycles. This led to the John Player International meetings, which were the prelude to the British Motorcycle Grand Prix, coming to Silverstone during the late 1970s and early 1980s. There was now a new crop of star names, too, like Barry Sheene, Mick Grant, Giacomo Agostini, Kent Andersson, Kork Ballington and Paul Smart.

But from the mid-1980s Silverstone shut its door to motorcycles, and they did not make a return until the beginning of the 1990s and the advent of the *Motor Cycle News* Superbike Championship series. Again there were more new names, including Terry Rymer, Carl Fogarty, John Reynolds, James Whitham and Brian Morrison.

From the end of the 1980s there seemed to be changes to the circuit every year; new bridges and tunnels; new pits; new press centre; the chicane, which replaced the old sweeping Woodcote section, in turn replaced by a dog-leg (some called it a dog's dinner – it was not liked by everyone!). Much of this change has been brought about by the Formula 1 car brigade, with Bernie Ecclestone forever saying that even these were not enough. In fact, at the beginning of the 21st century, even though more major changes had occurred Silverstone seemed under constant threat by Ecclestone to lose its ability to host the British Grand Prix (cars of course). And during the summer of 2008 this actually happened, with the British car GP to run at Donington from 2010.

1961 Hutchinson 100 programme.

1978 British Grand Prix programme.

As for motorcycle events, actual racing is almost non-existent with the exception of an occasional club event. This is something of a shame, although from a personal view Silverstone as it is now is not the Silverstone of old. In fact the 'paddock' is now more akin to an industrial estate, with its masses of concrete, bricks and mortar, while the circuit itself has now more and more become suited to four, rather than two wheels.

SYSTON

Syston road races at Syston Park, near Grantham, Lincolnshire, were probably the best of the early small road races and were used from 1926 until the mid-1930s.

Measuring some 1.75 miles (2.81km) to a lap, the races were run in a clockwise direction. The circuit was roughly triangular in shape. From the start the road rose gently to a right-hand turn, then ran along a hill top with a difficult downhill sweep to the right, dropped through a winding wooded section and what was described as a 'village street of estate buildings' (*The Motor Cycle*). Finally it fell away to a very sharp right-handed hairpin, the fast approach to which called for hard breaking, and thus back to the start again.

The biggest event of each year was the Grand Prix meeting, which normally attracted several star riders and large crowds. This was run by the Grantham and District Motor Cycle and Light Car club whose headquarters at the time were The George Hotel, Grantham. The president of the club was Sir John G. Thorgold, who just happened to also be the landowner of Syston Park.

Looking at the entry list from the Saturday 14 May 1932 programme, it can be seen that there were a total of 56 names, and included among these were Austin Munks, Sam Coupland, Harold Daniell, Maurice Cann, Arthur Tyler and Noel Mavrogordato.

WELLESBOURNE

Wellesbourne, or to give it its full name Wellesbourne Mountford, is situated some 5 miles (8km) east of Stratford-upon-Avon in Warwickshire. During the early–mid-1960s it was a well-known sprinting venue, the runway of the old airfield being used.

Later, an attempt was made to extend its use in motorcycle sport to include road racing, and events were run from the late 1960s until the late 1970s. Circuit length unknown.

Syston programme from 14 May 1932.

NORTH EAST

Barkston Heath (mid-1990s)
Beadnell (1956)
Brough (1947–56)
Cadwell Park (1930s–)
Carnaby (1970s)
Carnaby 2 (2001–04)
Catterick Airfield (1959–60)
Catterick Camp (1962–63)
Croft (1949–51, 1964–67, 1995–)
Dunholme (1947–48)
Elvington (1969–)
Esholt (1931–55)
Everthorpe Park (1947)
Langbaurgh (late 1980s, early 1990s)
Ormesby Hall (1936)
Ouston (1960–65)
Rufforth (1970s)
Scarborough (1946–)
Teesside Autodrome (2006–)
Thornaby (1959–61)
Tranwell (1950)
West Park (1935)

Programme from 1996.

Barkston Heath, mid-1990s.

BARKSTON HEATH

RAF Barkston Heath, between Grantham and Sleaford, Lincolnshire, was used by the local Pegasus MC and LCC during the mid-1990s for several years beginning in 1993. As the club acknowledged, this was due to the station commander of local RAF Cranwell who had kindly given them the facility. A stipulation was that no paying spectators were allowed. But as I was then running a race team, I was fortunate enough to attend the meeting held at Barkston Heath over the weekend of Saturday and Sunday 15 and 16 June 1996. This was true club

racing for sport rather than financial reward. The circuit length was just over one mile (1.61km) and was a typical airfield venue. There were around 25 races each day, with classes for both solos and sidecars.

BEADNELL

Beadnell, near Seahouses, Northumberland. This circuit was used only once, in the autumn of 1956. The meeting was organised by the Scottish-based Border Motor Racing Club. The race ran in a clockwise direction and its length is unknown. The circuit was abandoned due to disagreement between landowners.

BROUGH

Organised by the Blackburn Welfare Motor Club, the circuit was in essence an airfield belonging to the Blackburn Aircraft Company (later absorbed into BAC – British Aircraft Corporation). The first meeting was staged on Sunday 23 March 1947. Right through to the final meeting on Saturday 29 September 1956 Brough always seemed to attract many of the top riders. Situated to the west of Hull in East Yorkshire, for the first two seasons the course measured 0.65 miles (1.04km) and was roughly oblong in shape with one side kinking into bends; however, from the beginning of the 1949 season it was extended to measure 1.17 miles (1.88km).

Brough always attracted large crowds, this being helped by the fact that, even in its extended length layout, it was still compact enough for spectators to have riders in sight throughout the circuit.

For the first few years the main Brough stars were Denis Parkinson, Jack Brett, Colin Horn (solos) and Jackie Beeton (sidecars). In its revised form the start–finish line was situated about a quarter way along the appropriately named Runway Straight, which was itself about half a mile (0.8km) in length. At the end of the straight the track doubled back to the right at the Runway Hairpin, and another shorter straight led on to Brough Bend (a left), followed on shortly afterwards by the right of Perimeter Bend. Then

1949 programme and map.

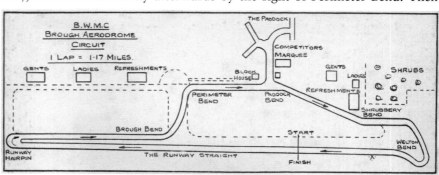

came the gentle right of Paddock Bend, next the slight curve of Shrubbery Bend. Finally there was the medium-right and sharp-right of Welton Bend, which led back to the Runway Straight.

Besides the main solo final being known as the Brough 25 at each season opener, another feature of the East Yorkshire venue was the inclusion of Formula 3 (500cc) cars at most of its meetings.

On Good Friday, 7 April 1950 Brough witnessed an infusion of new racing talent at the circuit with Bill Lomas winning the 250 and 350cc races on Enfield and Velocette machines respectively. The 500cc and Brough 25 finals saw a battle royal between George Brown (998cc Vincent HRD) and Sid Barnett (498cc Triumph) in both events, with Brown taking the honours at the end of each. George also set a new course record of 61.6mph (99.1km/h).

On Easter Saturday, 24 March 1951, Brough staged a race meeting as part of the Kingston-upon-Hull Festival of Britain celebrations. The main race of the day was for the Kingston-upon-Hull Trophy, donated by the municipal corporation. After a snowstorm during the morning, the weather brightened and there was sunshine – and racing – in the afternoon.

A notable entry was Geoff Duke on factory Nortons, but he was beaten in both the 350cc and Festival of Britain Championship races by Mick Featherstone (AJS) and course specialist Colin Horn (Norton) respectively.

Later that year every record was broken (including the attendance), when Bill Doran (works AJSs) and Jack Brett (works Nortons) clashed – Brett victorious in both the 350 and 500cc events – plus new class lap records.

Mick Featherstone (AJS 7R) leading the 350cc race at Brough Airfield, Easter Saturday, 1951. Number 12 is a KTT Velocette, number 2 Norton-mounted Geoff Duke.

Yorkshireman Denis
Parkinson at Brough in 1954
(Norton Manx).

As the 1950s unfolded, many of the top stars of the day visited Brough. None more so than John Surtees and that legendary Scottish duo of Bob McIntyre and Alastair King. At the first meeting of Brough's final year it was McIntyre who dominated the 250, 350cc and Brough 25 races, winning all three and setting the fastest lap in each. But it was to be Surtees who was to have the honour of being the outright Brough lap record holder (created on 4 April 1955) at 65.31mph (105.08km/h).

And so to that final meeting in October 1956. Increased air traffic was given as the reason why from then on Brough was unable to be used for racing, a sad day indeed; however, in its 10 seasons the Welfare Society of Blackburn Aircraft Company could be proud of its achievements in running a series of well-supported and well-run events.

The Norton outfit of Ernie
Walker (29) and Bill Boddice
at Brough Bend during a
1957 meeting at the East
Yorkshire track.

Cadwell Park c.1935, around the original Mountain Bend.

Programme from the re-opening of Cadwell Park, Easter 1946.

Allan Dudley-Ward with his JAP-engineered DW Special in the Cadwell Park paddock as it was in August 1946.

CADWELL PARK

In 1934 Cadwell Park, between Horncastle and Louth in the Lincolnshire Wolds, held its first motorcycle event as a dirt track. This was the brainchild of Charles Wilkinson, who two years earlier had formed the Louth and District Motor Cycle Club.

The Coronation Day race meeting in spring 1937 the meeting had to be abandoned owing to rain and the subsequent state of the course. So before the next event on August Bank Holiday Monday that year the organising club expanded considerable time and money improving the track.

The starting straight (still in use today) had been re-laid in rough-surfaced concrete, while the Hairpin had been similarly treated, and the sections which had already been concreted were widened. The race winners that day included Tommy Wood (Velocette) in the 350, 500 and Unlimited solo events and Jackie Beeton in the sidecars.

A crowd estimated between 12–15,000 saw England's first post-war motorcycle road races at Cadwell Park on Good Friday 1946.

Charles Wilkinson's father (and then owner of the Cadwell Park estate) was Monty Wilkinson, and he was accorded the honour of starting the historic first race of the post-war era. As *The Motor Cycle* race report said, 'The ¾ mile [1.2km] course was in almost as good

View of Cadwell Park,
Lincolnshire at the very first
post-war race meeting held
on 25 April 1946.

Cadwell Park, start, late
1950s.

condition as when the last rider finished his final circuit in August 1939.' Entries included Les Graham, Maurice Cann, Ronnie Mead, Doug Beasley, Tommy Wood, Eric Oliver, Allan Dudley-Ward, George Brown and Jack Surtees (father of John). The lap record of 52 seconds was broken on three occasions – by Oliver, Graham and finally Brown in exactly 50 seconds.

Throughout the remainder of the 1940s Cadwell remained a popular venue, with meetings every bank holiday weekend.

In the closed season of 1951–52 it was announced that plans had been submitted to the local authorities to extend the circuit to a length of 1.25 miles (2.01km). The original circuit, comprising the Mountain, Hall Bends, Hairpin Corner and Barn Corner, would be extended from the end of the start–finish straight by adding a neck and then rejoining the existing circuit near the first part of the Mountain section.

The first use of the extended circuit came on August Bank Holiday Monday 1952, but before this Peter Davey became the ultimate lap record holder of the original circuit with a time of 44.8 seconds.

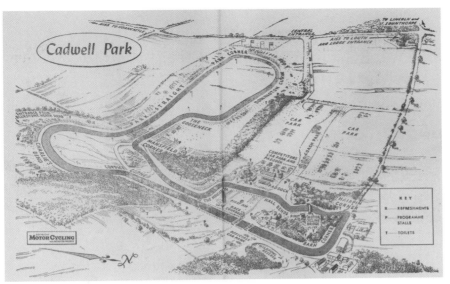

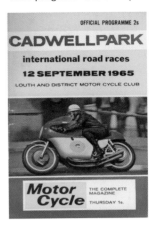

1965 programme and map.

Next in June 1960, came news that Cadwell was to be extended yet again to 2.25 miles (3.62km), the longer circuit was first used on August Bank Holiday Monday 1961. Quickest to weigh up the new track (which remains much the same today) was Dennis Pratt who, with 350 and 500cc Nortons, repeated his double wins at the Easter and Whitsun meetings on the old circuit. The new sections included Park Straight, the Gooseneck and Mansfield corner.

Probably the heyday of the Lincolnshire course came during the late 1960s and early 1970s when all the world's top stars visited Cadwell,

Cadwell Park, mid-1960s, a group of Manx Nortons drop down from the Gooseneck to Mansfield Corner.

Giacomo Agostini cresting Cadwell's Mountain, international meeting, September 1970.

Cadwell Park 1977.
American Pat Hennan leads
Barry Sheene, Dave Potter
and Mick Grant.

Joey Dunlop (Honda RS500
triple), Cadwell Park, April
1984.

A Pro-Am (Yamaha LC)
event at Cadwell Park in
1984, on the downward
approach to Mansfield
Corner.

including John Cooper, Mike Hailwood, Bill Ivy, Giacomo Agostini, Phil Read and many others; however, it was local rider Derek Chatterton who was often the victor. Crowds of over 60,000 would flock to the picturesque Lincolnshire circuit.

During the 1980s and 1990s the full Grand Prix 2.25-mile circuit was restricted to mainly the bigger meetings, with the shorter Club and Woodlands circuits playing host to the club events.

Cadwell Park, 1992. Dave
Eastough (Suzuki RGV250)
leads a clubman's Super
Sport 400 race on the
approach to the Mountain.

Dean Johnson cresting the Mountain at Cadwell on his Fowler-Yamaha TZ250, British Championship meeting, August 1996.

However, at the beginning of the 21st century the vast majority of events are held on the full circuit but a chicane has been placed on what was previously the straight section between the Mansfield and the approach to the Mountain in an attempt to slow riders at the latter point.

After more than 50 years Charles Wilkinson decided to call it a day, and he accepted an offer from the Brands Hatch group at the end of the 1970s. Charles eventually moved to Dorchester with his wife Pat. Today the circuit is owned by Motor Vision organisation, headed by Jonathan Palmer. This same organisation also controls Brands Hatch, Oulton Park and Snetterton.

The big motorcycle meeting in the current Cadwell calendar is the British Superbike round, traditionally run over the August Bank Holiday weekend.

On a personal note, Cadwell, together with Snetterton, is my local circuit, and both I and my son Gary raced there on many occasions. I have even had a meeting, the 1978 May Day National, named after me!

CARNABY RACEWAY

Carnaby Raceway, Bridlington, East Yorkshire, came about thanks to the Auto 66 club wanting to own its own road race circuit. In the early 1970s the club successfully applied for planning permission and opened the one-and-a-half-mile (2.41km) track. Although critics had said it would not work, they were proved wrong as the venture was a roaring success, with even a number of British Championship meetings. In fact, at one the BBC televised the British Championship live for two days – the only event other than a Grand Prix in the UK to have two days' live coverage.

2008 programme.

Club rider M. Hepworth racing his virtually standard Kawasaki Z1 at Carnaby, Yorkshire, August 1976.

1975 programme.

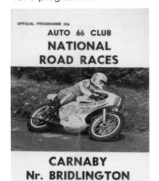

OFFICIAL PROGRAMME 20p

AUTO 66 CLUB
**NATIONAL
ROAD RACES**

**CARNABY
Nr. BRIDLINGTON**
Sunday, 3rd Aug., 1975

Carnaby raceway. Nick Andrews, Auto 66 Club champion (Suzuki GSX 1100), in the production class, 1981.

The Auto 66 club also ran RAC British Car Sprint Championships and Kart Championships at Carnaby Raceway before the East Yorkshire Borough Council decided that they wanted to develop the site for industrial purposes.

The mid-1970s was Carnaby's heyday, with a host of star riders taking part.

1982, Dave Davis, (Maxton Yamaha), 500cc Auto 66 Championship winner.

Mark Westmorland (189) and Roy Goodhall battle it out at Carnaby on 18 April 1982.

These included Tony Rutter, Phil Mellor, Austin Hockley, Paul Cott, Nick Jefferies, Roger Marshall, George Fogarty, Peter McKindlay, Tony Smith and Nigel Stone.

CARNABY TWO

The 2001 season was successful for the East Yorkshire-based Auto 66 Club which organised a number of meetings at the new Carnaby Two circuit. Located at Leconfield (a former Royal Air Force station now used for heavy goods vehicle training), situated a couple of miles to the north of Beverley, Carnaby Two was strictly a club circuit, unlike its earlier, more well-known Bridlington namesake.

CATTERICK AIRFIELD

Confusingly, there were two Catterick circuits – one was the RAF airfield, the other the army camp. The former came first, with a meeting on Sunday 12 July 1959. Organised by the Yorkshire Centre ACU and the Darlington and District Motor Club, the circuit was roughly triangular in shape and ran in a clockwise direction. Measuring 1.6 miles (2.5km) in total, there was a 0.7-mile (1.1km) long straight followed by the sharp hairpin Dicers' Delight, then passing the pits the next section was The Snake, followed by Far North Corner. The next straight, 0.4 miles (0.6km) in length, ran beside the Great North Road (A1), and at the end of this was another hairpin Hanger Corner, which exited into the main straight and thus the end of the lap.

Programme from 1959.

Official Programme
1/-
DARLINGTON & DISTRICT MOTOR CLUB LTD.
ROAD RACES
At CATTERICK AIRFIELD
SUNDAY, 12th JULY, 1959

MOTORCYCLE NEWS
4D. EVERY WEDNESDAY

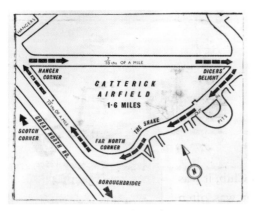

Circuit map from 1959.

Alan Shepherd was the star man at the July 1959 Catterick Airfield meeting, winning the 350cc final on an AJS 7R and the 500cc final on a Matchless G50.

One hundred and sixty-eight entries were received for the next meeting at the airfield circuit on Sunday 26 June 1960, but this time it was the 250cc final which caught the eye with a four-way scrap for the lead between Jack Murgatroyd (NSU), R. West (203 MV Agusta), Brian Clark (175 Ducati) and Bill Crosier (Velocette). After West crashed, Murgatroyd went on to snatch victory from Crosier and Clark.

CATTERICK CAMP

The second Catterick circuit was the 1.2-mile (1.9km) army camp course which held its first meeting on Sunday 2 September 1962. It packed no less than 15 tight corners into the lap and was too narrow for sidecars and too sinuous for 500cc machines, so it catered for 50, 200, 250 and 350cc solos. Some 5,000 spectators saw three hours of heats before the racing proper got under way. The winners of these were 50cc Alan Dawson (Pope Special), 125 and 200cc Ken Martin (Bultacos), 250cc John Ashworth (Aermacchi) and 350cc Rob Fitton (AJS).

The circuit ran in an anti-clockwise direction, and if one studies the map it is possible to see that this was an ideal venue for the smallest machines but less suitable with capacity rise.

Racing continued there for the 1963 season, and at the end of August approximately 10,000 spectators saw some close racing. The race winners

Programme and circuit map from Catterick Camp, 1962.

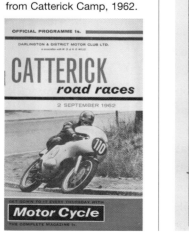

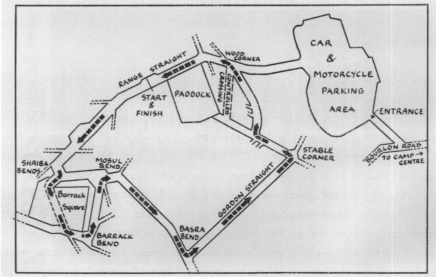

this time were 50cc Dave Simmonds (Tohatsu), 125cc Carl Ward (Honda), 200cc Ken Martin (Bultaco) and 250cc Stan Wright (Aermacchi). No 350cc were catered for.

CROFT

Croft, a former World War Two Royal Air Force Bomber Command station some five miles south of Darlington, held its first motorcycle race meeting on 20 August 1949. The 1.33-mile (2.13km) circuit made use of the existing runway and perimeter track. Organised by the local Darlington Club, it was open to Yorkshire Centre ACU members. This original circuit was often known as Neasham, rather than Croft, in the very early days.

A second meeting was held on 20 May 1950 and a third on 19 August 1950. By the first meeting of 1951, held in early May, the circuit length had been increased to some 2.25 miles (3.62km). Then Croft was lost to racing when the Royal Air Force returned to establish the airfield as an emergency landing strip.

In December 1963, however, news came through that racing was to return the following year. In July 1964 it was revealed that over the previous four months a new company had spent over £40,000 laying a newly surfaced 1.75-mile (2.81km) circuit. This was Croft Autodrome, and it was tried out by John Cooper and John Sear in July that year, prior to the inaugural meeting for bikes and cars on August Bank Holiday Monday, 3 August 1964. There were three 12-lap races with 250cc, 500cc and sidecars, won by Eddie Johnson (Aermacchi), Dave Reid (Norton) and Colin Appleyard (Triumph) respectively. Reid set the fastest lap at 74.69mph (120.17km/h).

Croft Autodrome continued to run regular meetings, and by 18 June 1966 John Cooper had raised the lap record to 77.40mph (124.53km/h) on his 499cc Norton.

On Saturday 17 September 1966 the North East Motor Cycle Racing Club organised a national event which attracted the likes of world champion Phil Read, Cadwell ace Derek Chatterton, the Australian Kevin Cass, plus leading northern and Scottish riders, including John Kiddie, Steve Murray, Brian Richards, Bill Crosier, Trevor Burgess, Alex George, Don Padgett, Rob Fitton, George Buchan, Ken Redfern and many more. There were no less than 42 sidecar crews, notably Mac Hobson and Owen Greenwood.

Although Croft Autodrome continued to hold car events until as late as 1981, motorcycle racing did not continue beyond the early 1970s. It reopened as Croft Circuit in 1995, only slightly different from its previous layout. After a two-year time span, it was turned into a modern, well-appointed facility with excellent amenities. Most of the old circuit, except

Croft programme and map from 1950. This is the original Neasham/Croft airfield circuit used in the early years; originally 1.33 miles (1949) and extended to 2.25 miles (3.62km) from 1951.

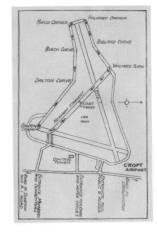

Programme and circuit map from 1966, showing the new layout, opened in 1964.

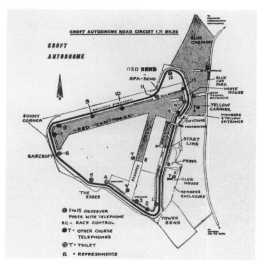

Croft programme from 1996.

Elvington programme from 1975.

for Railway Straight, was retained, but there was now what is best described as an inner complex, which includes a new start–finish. The length is now 2.13 miles (3.32km) and, as before, runs in a clockwise direction.

These improvements were primarily made so that Croft could host the BTCC Touring Cars; however, this in turn worked in motorcycle racing's favour too, as by the beginning of the 21st century Croft became a venue for a round of the British Superbike Championship. For the last few years this has remained very much the case.

Certainly, Croft has become the sports premier circuit in the North East of England, and long may this state of affairs continue. It has even been used as a stage for the RAC car rally.

ELVINGTON

In 1969 the Auto 66 Club gained the use of RAF Elvington, some five miles (8.045km) east of York. The first motorcycle road race meeting was held on Sunday 31 August 1969. This was over a 1.9-mile (3km) circuit watched by a crowd of 7,000 spectators. The main 1000cc race was won by Tony Jefferies (750 Norton).

The National meeting in 1971 attracted one of the largest entries ever seen in the north of England, with well over 400 competitors, including up-and-coming stars Tony Jefferies, Mick Grant and Barry Sheene.

During the early days at Elvington the Eboracum Motor Club of York also staged motorcycle race meetings at Elvington. A typical Eboracum programme was the meeting held on 24 May 1975. This featured classes for 50/125, 250, 350, 500, 1000cc, Sidecars, Production, Vintage and Unlimited Solos. Among the entry list was Phil Mellor and Stu Rogers (the latter racing a 1939 490cc Norton in the Vintage class).

Vee Pickering (250cc Yamaha) TZ double winner at Elvington on 4 April 1982.

The site is still being used by the Auto 66 Club today, some 38 years after its 1970 debut. There are two circuits, known as Elvington Park National (with corner names after northern motorcycle heroes – Padgetts, Jefferies, Grants, Websters and Cronshaws) and Elvington Park Club. The former has a lap measuring 1.7 miles (2.73km), whereas the latter is precisely one mile (1.61km).

ESHOLT

The Esholt Park circuit, near Bradford, began at Easter 1931 with meetings organised by the Bradford Special Constables Association Motor Section. This first outing drew vast crowds, over 50,000 in fact!

As can be seen from a map of the course, which was just over 1.75 miles (2.81km) in length, it consisted of a dead straight avenue, and over a quarter of a mile on this section sprint events were held in the early days, as well as the conventional circuit.

For 1932 there was only one Esholt meeting, since the venue, which was the property of the Bradford Corporation, was not always available. But what an entry, with a host of star riders including the likes of Ted Mellors (later multi-European Champion) and Tommy Spann to name but two.

Originally billed as the 'Tourist Trophy Races' for the 1932 event and thereafter known as the 'Open Speed Races', Esholt Park continued to attract top-

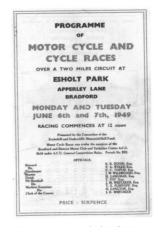

Programme and circuit map from 1949.

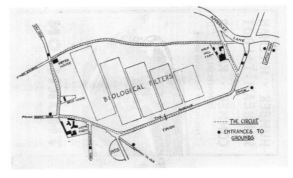

Circuit map from the 1952
programme.

line riders throughout the remainder of the 1930s such as Freddie Frith, Maurice Cann and Yorkshire's own Allan Jefferies from nearby Shipley.

Then came the war, and there was no more motorcycle sport at Esholt until 1948 when a sprint was organised on Easter Tuesday (a local holiday both sides of the war), with racing resuming on August Bank Holiday that same year.

On Easter Monday 1949 a crowd exceeding 15,000 saw battles between Denis Parkinson and Allan Jefferies. Then, a couple of months later, on Whit Monday, Jefferies scored a hat-trick of victories, which was to begin that rider's virtual monopoly at Esholt Park.

Until the end of the 1951 season everything had gone smoothly over the years for the popular West Yorkshire venue – large crowds, exciting racing and no serious injuries. But things were about to go into reverse. The first setback came in June 1952, when the meeting clashed with the local Lancashire–Yorkshire cricket match, and the War of the Roses won. This saw a poor attendance at Esholt, even though Denis Parkinson debuted one of the new Featherbed Nortons, with which he took his customary victory.

Next came a massive crash at the Easter 1953 meeting, when half the field came to grief in the 500cc race, resulting in one fatality and a trio of serious injuries.

But the organisers, now the Eccleshall and Undercliff Memorial Hall Fund, the riders and spectators all rallied round to make the Easter 1954 races a big commercial success. At the end of that year Denis Parkinson retired and local rider Ben Denton (Norton) assumed Parkinson's position as the star turn that year. Unfortunately, 1955 was to provide Esholt Park's final season. This was due to the ACU withholding a permit for 1956 as they considered parts of the circuit were not up to standard. Resurfacing was needed, but discussions between the Memorial Hall Fund Committee and Bradford Corporation failed to resolve the funding problem, and so after a quarter of a century Esholt Park was lost to the racing world.

An interesting footnote is that today the village of Esholt is the location for the popular Yorkshire Television series *Emmerdale* – so it still attracts the public!

EVERTHORPE PARK

In July 1947 Hull Motor Club organised a road race meeting at Everthorpe Park, which was adjacent to the main road and lay halfway between Hull and Goole. The circuit was three-fifths of a mile (0.96km) in length and consisted of the main and rear gravel drives leading to and round the hall, plus grass which received the attention of a motor roller before the actual racing. The organising secretary was none other than Charles Wilkinson of Cadwell Park fame.

The 24 July 1947 issue of *The Motor Cycle* described the inaugural Everthorpe Park meeting as, 'English parkland; a stately house which is almost a castle; loud speakers stuck like gargoyles on cemented parapets; music, trees, crowds, sunshine – these all formed the setting for the Hull Motor Club's enjoyable open-to-Centre races at Everthorpe Park, near Goole, last Saturday.' There were six races in total but without any riders of particular note.

The second meeting, held in mid-August the same year, featured improvements by way of tarmac being laid at Hall Bend and on a portion of the straight.

The third and final meeting of 1947 was adjudged to have been the best and included some 'star' riders, including Eric Oliver and Tommy Wood. There is no record of meetings taking place after this date.

LANGBAURGH

Langbaurgh on Teesside in north-east England was the location for a very successful Euro Challenge Super Moto event in 1989, staged by the go-ahead Auto 66 Club. Unfortunately, although very popular in continental Europe, Super Moto in Britain did not catch on at the time so this event was not repeated; however, Langbaurgh did host a number of club level road racing meetings during the late 1980s and early 1990s.

ORMESBY HALL

Ormesby Hall was an estate on the outskirts of Middlesbrough and featured a continuous road circuit of one and a half miles (2.41km).

The local Middlesbrough Club held an 'experimental' race meeting there at the beginning of September 1936. It was a far-from-perfect venue as, although one side was tarmac, the other, as *The Motor Cycle* described 'was a rather greasy surfaced pathway through a shrubbery, where overtaking would be nigh impossible'. There were three races, 350cc, 600cc and a 30-mile (48.2km) Handicap, plus a 'consolation' event for non-winners. Jack Brett was the most notable rider, winning the 350cc (Velocette) and finishing runner-up in the 600cc event.

Ouston programme and circuit map.

OUSTON

RAF station Ouston was used for a number of race meetings, organised jointly by the Newcastle and District Motor Club and the Border Motor Racing Club, from 1960 until 1965. Situated some seven miles (11km) west of Newcastle-upon-Tyne, the circuit ran in a clockwise direction and was one and a half miles (2.4km) in length.

From the start the course ran down to Crossways followed by Hillhead. Then came a long curve, which eventually was slowed down by The Esses and the almost hairpin-like Cheeseburn, before exiting onto the start–finish line to complete the lap. All corners, with the exception of The Esses, were right-handers.

Large crowds, sometimes in excess of 30,000, attended these meetings, and there were equally large entries. For example, on Sunday 18 June 1961 over 270 motorcycles took part. The race winners that day were 125cc Gary Dickinson (Ducati), 200cc Brian Clark (Ducati), 250cc Dennis Gallagher (Velocette), 350cc and 500cc Dennis Pratt (Nortons), with the two sidecar events both being won by T.C. Layton (998cc Vincent HRD). Dennis Pratt and Jack Bullock (Norton) jointly set the fastest lap in the 500cc race with a speed of 83.03mph (133.59km/h).

In March 1966 it was announced that the planned national meeting scheduled for 19 June that year would not take place. As this was a joint car and motorcycle event, the RAC had refused a permit because there were no permanent safety barriers necessary for four-wheelers, and as Ouston was an operational airfield this was impossible.

At first it had been thought that the motorcycle part of the meeting might continue, but the RAF then withdrew permission. So racing at Ouston came to an untimely end, and the club was left trying to locate an alternative venue in the North East which proved extremely difficult for a Sunday event.

RUFFORTH

Rufforth, between York and Wetherby, was the venue for a combined car and motorcycle meeting, the two-wheel side being organised by the Auto 66 Club. Unfortunately an injunction at 6pm the previous evening saw the bikes excluded – and a lot of unhappy racers!

Although Rufforth has played host to cars on numerous occasions, bikes have never returned.

SCARBOROUGH

In the five years leading up to the outbreak of World War Two on 3 September 1939, members of the Scarborough and District Motor Club were very active in attempting to bring road racing to the local district. The preferred site was a 14-mile (22.5km) circuit at Seamer Moor, near the north-east Yorkshire seaside resort. A rival venue was a 10-mile (16.1km) course on the town's former racecourse, but nothing had been firmly decided by the time Mr Hitler went into war mode.

When peace finally returned in 1945 the club, together with the Yorkshire centre of the ACU and the Borough Council, immediately began a search for a venue where racing could be staged within the locality. Cost was a consideration, and the site eventually chosen was a 2.41-mile (3.88km) circuit on the picturesque wooded slopes of Oliver's Mount on the southern edge of the town.

Constructed in record-breaking time, the circuit was officially opened in mid-September 1946. At the first meeting a couple of days later the competition got under way with practising and racing for 350cc machines on Tuesday 17 September, with practice for the 500cc the following day and racing on the Thursday.

The start and finish (for the first two meetings only) was midway between the Esses. From there riders proceeded in an anti-clockwise direction to Memorial Corner, then to Mount Hairpin, followed by Mountside Hairpin, after which came the downhill blast to Mere Hairpin and from there back up the steep incline to the Esses and the start of a new lap. All these vantage points remain on the circuit in the 21st century.

The man generally acknowledged to be the father of Scarborough racing was Jack Claxton, who was in charge for that first meeting in 1946 through to his eventual retirement in September 1965.

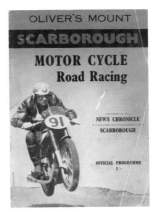

Oliver's Mount programme, 1949.

Oliver's Mount programme and map from 1951.

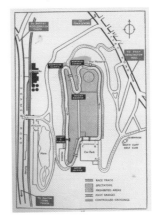

Start of 500cc final, September 1950. Number 24 is Maurice Cann, 99 Bob Foster and 8 Geoff Duke.

Scarborough, 31 August 1968, Memorial Corner. 18 Rob Fitton (499 Norton), 11 Barry Randle (499 Norton).

Oliver's Mount programme and map from 1965.

Barry Sheene, Scarborough, 3 September 1977 negotiating the jumps on Bottom Straight.

Oliver's Mount soon captured the imagination of race fans and holiday-goers alike. So popular did the meetings become that BBC Radio commentaries were broadcast nationwide from 1947 onwards, and a couple of these commentators were father and son Graham and Murray Walker. From the start Oliver's Mount also attracted the top riders of the day, and in early years these included Denis Parkinson, George Brown, and Sid Barnett. These were soon to be followed by future world champions Eric Oliver, Geoff Duke, Cecil Sandford and Bill Lomas.

From 1947, racing transferred to Fridays and Saturdays. In fact Sunday racing did not begin at Scarborough until 1971.

Between 1946 and the circuit's 50th Anniversary Meeting in September 1996, a total of 123 race meetings had been staged at Oliver's Mount. Of these 47 had been full internationals, 74 were nationals, and in both 1985 and 1986 a 'Festival of Yesteryear' was held.

Dickie Dale in July 1949 became the first rider to win three finals in a single weekend when he took the flag in the 250, 350 and 500cc events. John Cooper was the first competitor to be victorious in four finals in a single day with wins in the 250, 350, 500 and 750cc Superbike classes in September 1971. But of course progress continues apace. Rob Orme won six races during the Gold Cup weekend in 1990, both legs of the 125cc National, both of the 125cc International, and one leg each of the 250cc Phil Mellor Trophy and International 250cc 'Prince of the Roads.' Second places in the two other legs gave him a total of six individual race wins with overall victory in four separate categories; however, in the first 50 years it was Carl Fogarty in September 1989 who notched up the best figures with an unbeaten seven race victories and four category wins.

During the late 1950s and early 1960s Scarborough was graced by men such as, in the first instance, John Surtees, Alan Shepherd, John Hartle and Bob McIntyre; followed by Dan Shorey, Mike Hailwood, John Cooper and Percy Tait, plus all the top sidecar men, including Florian Camathias, Helmut Fath, Pip Harris, Fritz Schneidegger and Max Deubel. Between 1957 and 1968 ABC Television (Yorkshire TV) often visited the Mount.

During the late 1960s and into the 1970s yet more star names made their mark at the Yorkshire venue. These included Barry Sheene, Jarno Saarinen, Phil Read, Giacomo Agostini, Tepi Lansivouri, Mick Grant, Will Hartog, Pat Hennen, Dave Croxford, Peter Williams and many, many more.

Barry Sheene (7) Yamaha, leads Bob Smith. Gold Cup International meeting, September 1980.

50th Anniversary programme from 1996.

Into the late 1970s and early 1980s, still more big names arrived such as Wayne Gardner, Graeme Crosby, Takazumi Katayama, Charlie Williams, Joey Dunlop, Rob McElnea and Keith Heuwen. But of these it was Mick Grant (still riding well into the 1980s) who was probably the most successful at Scarborough during the 1970s and 1980s. Another rider, Phil Mellor, was also the winner of a record number of Scarborough finals from 1980 onwards until his untimely death in the TT later that decade.

The next big names during the late 1980s and early 1990s were James Whitham and Carl Fogarty. Into the present time it has been Chris Palmer, Dean Ashton, Ian Lougher and, most latterly, Guy Martin.

Besides the changing picture of riding talent, there have been notable changes to the circuit. The first came in September 1947 when the start–finish line was moved to its present location (see map). Then in 1954 major widening and resurfacing was undertaken. In 1956 the present Race Control Tower was built (then the most modern in Europe), and in May 1991 the

The approach to the start–finish line at Oliver's Mount, Scarborough, c.1990.

Programme from July 2007.

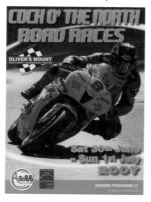

Teesside Autodrome programme, 2007.

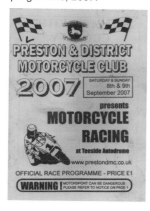

introduction of the Farm Bends section saw an increase in length from 2.41 miles (3.86km) to 2.43 miles (3.91km).

And so Scarborough lives on, and somehow it has retained the charisma of great days gone by – something most other circuits seem to have lost over the years. It is certainly one of my favourites, and I am always made welcome by Peter Hillaby and his Auto 66 Club team.

TEESSIDE AUTODROME

Teesside Autodrome (or to give it its full name South Tees Motor Sport Park) is situated near the South Bank of the River Tees in Middlesbrough. Opened in 2006, it is one of Britain's newest circuits and has brought motorcycle racing to the Teesside area.

Owned and operated by ex-professional racing driver Bob Pope, Teesside Autodrome is also a major centre for kart racing; in fact it can at 2.4 miles (3.86km) lay claim to being the world's longest karting venue. In the complex there are embodied other, shorter, circuit choices.

So far bike racing has been confined to club events, notably organised by the Preston and District Club, but hopefully national, or even international, meetings can be organised in the future.

Motorcycle events are currently held over the one-mile (1.61km) club circuit, incorporating a long straight with the tight South Bend and Cleveland at either end, and with the stadium section incorporating Pope's and The Kink running parallel to the aforementioned straight.

THORNABY

Glorious weather, a large entry, and some keenly contested races were the ingredients for the Middlesbrough and District MC successful race meeting at Thornaby Airfield, North Yorkshire, on Sunday 9 August 1959. There were classes for 250, 350, Unlimited and the East Yorks Championship Handicap – all held over 10 laps of the 1.9-mile (3km) course. The final meeting at Thornaby took place two years later on 20 August 1961; Peter Bettison (Manx Nortons) scoring a fine double.

TRANWELL

The Newcastle club held an open to centre road race meeting at Tranwell Airfield, Morpeth, Northumberland, on Sunday 10 September 1950 with proceeds going to the Royal Air Force Benevolent Fund. The circuit measured one and a half miles (2.41km). A total of 79 entries appeared in the programme, with classes for 125, 200, 250, 350, 1000cc and sidecars. Among the 'star' riders were George Brown (499 and 998cc Vincent HRD) and George Todd (123cc BSA).

Tranwell programme and circuit map, 1950.

WEST PARK

West Park, Hull in East Yorkshire, was the setting on Saturday 6 July 1935 for a race meeting to raise funds in aid of the local British Legion (for veterans of World War One).

The parkland circuit, measuring 0.665 miles (1.069km), was used by permission of Hull City Corporation. It was organised jointly by Hull, Horsforth and District, Hull Auto, Scarborough, Sheffield, Hallamshire and York Motor Club.

Commencing at 6.15pm (to allow for those who had been working during the day to attend), the top performer was local rider H.B. (Herbert) Myers.

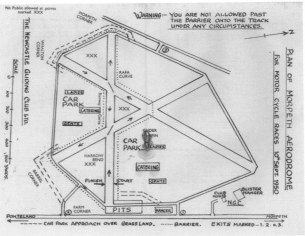

NORTH WEST

Aintree (1954–)
Altcar (1947–55)
Belle Vue (1927–28)
Flookburgh (early 1980s)
Greeves Hall Project (late 1930s)
Longridge (1974–78)
New Brighton (1960–1980s)
Oulton Park (1953–)
Parbold (1930s)
Silloth (1964–78, 1981–83)
Three Sisters (early 1990s–)

AINTREE

In early September 1954 Geoff Duke, together with a host of other top-line riders, met Mrs Muriel Topham, the owner of the new Aintree motor racing circuit near Liverpool, and gave their approval of the course which was due to stage its first motorcycle meeting later that month.

This inaugural event took place on Saturday 25 September, organised by the North Western Centre of the ACU and sponsored by the *Daily Telegraph* newspaper.

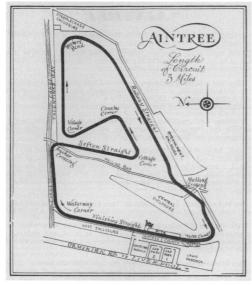

Circuit map from 1954.

Among the entries for the 500cc race were the Gileras of Reg Armstrong and Duke, Ray Amm and Jack Brett (Nortons), Rod Coleman, Bob McIntyre and Derek Farrant (AJSs) and the sole MV Agusta of Dickie Dale, no less than eight pukka works bikes.

The Aintree circuit measured three miles (4.8km) to a lap and ran side-by-side with the world-famous Grand National racecourse. Completed in May that year at a cost said to have been in excess of £100,000 (many millions in today's values), there was stand accommodation for 20,000 spectators while the total capacity for the circuit was said to be in the region of 200,000.

The meeting was held in dry but windy conditions. The main race was over 20 laps, or 60 miles (96.5km),

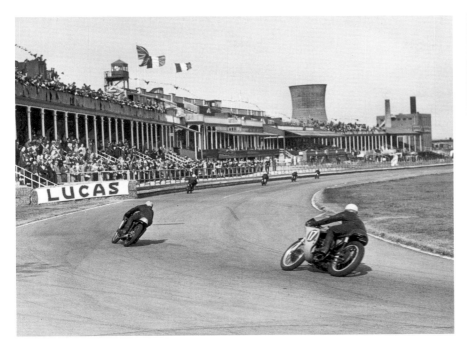

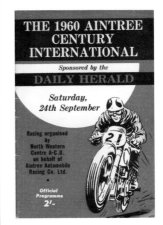

Aintree International 26 September 1959, number 17 Dan Shorey (348cc Norton).

Programme cover from 1960.

and it developed into a battle royal between the two Gileras and privateer John Surtees (Norton). The latter made a tremendous start and went away 'like a shot from a gun' (*The Motor Cycle*). Although both Armstrong and Duke had passed Surtees by the end of the second lap, this was far from the end of the matter. Surtees did not give up and promptly slipstreamed Armstrong's Gileras. Eventually Surtees overtook Armstrong and then began to draw slowly away. Meanwhile, Duke had kept a wary eye on the happenings astern and placed himself with a respectable distance to the good at the front with the fastest lap of the race at 81.5mph (131.24km/h). By the end of the race Duke had proved to have complete mastery – quite simply in 1954 no one on the planet could match the combination of him and the four cylinder Gilera.

As for Aintree, somehow it never managed to get near the success levels for motorcycle racing as it did as a horse racing venue. Although for the remainder of the 1950s it continued to attract many of the world's top stars, spectators were always at a premium. By the early 1960s Aintree as an international motorcycle racing circuit had long since ended.

The Aintree Club Circuit.

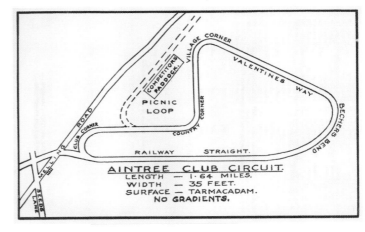

Programme from 2008.

Programme and map from 1949.

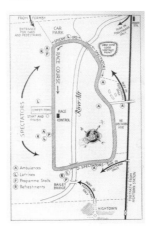

As a shorter club circuit it fared better, however, the shorter course being 1.64 miles (2.63km). Both national, and club events were held there during the 1970s.

On Saturday 27 May 1978, the Aintree Grand National took place with many of the UK's top stars of the day, including Roger Marshall, Ron Haslam, Tony Rutter, John Newbold, Mick Grant and Charlie Williams. This was in fact the first national meeting at Aintree for over 20 years. By the 1980s, however, Aintree had returned to club racing, a position that continues to the present day; thanks in no small part to the efforts of Dave Edwards, chairman of the Aintree Motor Cycle Racing Club.

Altcar

Road racing (or, more accurately, path racing) began at the Altcar rifle range, organised by the Waterloo club on 16 August 1947. The course was situated near Formby, between Liverpool and Southport, and was one and a half miles (2.4km) in length. Roughly rectangular, with one side comprising a well-surfaced straight of just under 0.5 miles (0.8km) in length, when first opened there were not only several very acute corners and S-bends, but the surface was extremely bumpy and loose – about half being dirt (which produced dust-clouds) and the remainder rolled ashes; the general width being between eight and 12ft.

The right to use the rifle range facilities was granted by the Territorial Association, with profit going to the Soldiers', Sailors' and Airmen's Families Association.

For this first meeting so many spectators turned up that the judges', officials' and competitors' enclosures were also overcrowded, slowing down the organisation of the meeting. Among the original entries were the likes of Tommy Wood, Bill Doran, Sid Barnett, Frank Fletcher and George Leigh. To give an idea of the difficult nature of the track, unofficial timing indicated lap speeds of between 36–38mph (58–61km/h) for the top men.

By the beginning of the 1950s the track surface had been completely concreted or tarmaced. There was also a new Bailey Bridge in place of the original North Bridge over the River Alt.

The definitive Altcar saw the original 0.5-mile (0.8km) straight, and at its end the course turned left over the South Bridge, and in a short distance left again at Railway Corner (so named due to the closeness of Hightown Station). After this there were some quickish left and right sweeps at Guard Corner and Farm Bend to the Bailey Bridge and then a final bend at Park Corner leading on to the finishing straight. The course ran in an anti-clockwise direction.

Only one meeting was staged in 1950, this taking place on 22 July with some 10,000 spectators. Had the weather been better it had been expected the crowd would have been considerably larger as Altcar always attracted a large number of spectators due to a lack of circuits in the North West.

An example of how much of an improvement had been made is to record that the 350cc race winner, Denis Parkinson (Norton) averaged 55.21mph (88.83km/h) for race distance.

A feature of the 1952 meeting, held as a Merseyside Festival of Britain attraction, was the appearance of Geoff Duke as a travelling marshal riding his 1949 Senior Clubman's TT-winning Norton International machine loaned by its present owner.

Two meetings were scheduled for 1953 in April and September. The first took place, but on the last lap of the last race a rider (known to the author, but not named) ran into the crowd at Railway corner and a spectator was killed. Even though the September meeting was subsequently cancelled, however, racing continued at Altcar throughout 1954 and 1955. After this the Waterloo Club transferred their meetings to other venues.

BELLE VUE

Organised by the North Manchester Motor Club in 1927 and 1928, Belle Vue road racing should not be confused with the Belle Vue Speedway team's activities, or for that matter the Belle Vue Classic Bike Show of the 1980s.

Instead, Belle Vue the race circuit was staged in parkland adjacent to a big mansion house in that area of Manchester. In the two years this event took place the most successful rider was TT winner Charlie Dodson (Sunbeam). The circuit was under one mile (1.61km) in length.

FLOOKBURGH

During the early 1980s the Barnsley, South Yorkshire-based Formula Five club ran a series of meetings at the Ponderosa, Flookburgh, Cumbria circuit.

During 1983 there were meetings on 10 April, 1 May, 12 June, 3 July and 7 August. At the first of these dates there were no less than 24 races for solos and sidecars. Among the entries were Kevin Mawdsley and Ian Duffus.

MOTORCYCLE ROAD RACING

PONDEROSA CIRCUIT

FLOOKBURGH

A Formula 5 Motorcycle Racing Club (Barnsley) Ltd., promotion

Cover Photo: PHIL MELLOR

Flookburgh programme, 1983.

Graham Cannell (Yamaha) in a Formula 5 club race at Flookburgh, Ocober 1981.

Riders waiting to go to start at Flookburgh on one of the all-too-rare sunny days in 1981.

GREEVES HALL PROJECT

An interesting, but ultimately unsuccessful, project for a substantial circuit was at Greeves Hall, between Southport and Preston, Lancashire.

The total length was 2.25 miles (3.62km). Within a 50-mile (80.5km) radius was a population of many millions with Manchester, Liverpool and a multitude of smaller industrial towns such as Blackburn, Bolton and Ormskirk.

It was hoped racing would take place there in 1937 – unfortunately this promising venue was to remain a pipe-dream only.

LONGRIDGE

On Sunday 12 May 1974 a new circuit at Longridge, near Preston, was opened by none other than six-times world champion Geoff Duke. As the Fleetwood and District Motor Cycle Club said in its programme of that day, 'Our grateful thanks to Geoff Duke OBE for coming over from the Isle of Man to open our first meeting at Longridge. His support and interest in the sport is an example to us all.'

A total of 111 solo entries took part in that first meeting, together with 17 sidecar crews. Interesting names included the veteran Eric Cheers, Brian 'Snowy' Cammock, Mick Baybutt plus the Sports Motorcycles duo of Steve Wynne and John Sear. A second meeting that year was held on Sunday 15 September.

The circuit length was 0.43 miles (0.69km) and ran in a clockwise direction. It was basically two hairpins, with an S-bend between the start and the first hairpin.

Longridge was unique in the annals of motor racing circuits as it was situated in a quarry. The circuit survived until the end of 1978, and although there were plans for racing in 1979 these were to remain unfilled as the site was sold off.

NEW BRIGHTON

For many years, from the 1960s to the 1980s the Wirral Hundred Motor Club staged road race meetings on the King's Parade, New Brighton Promenade, Wallasey, Merseyside.

The first-ever meeting took place on Saturday 10 September 1960 watched by a crowd of some 5,000 spectators. This unfamiliar setting on the public highway was only made possible by a special road-closing Act of Parliament backed by the local Wallasey Corporation.

At just over one mile (1.61km) to a lap, the course required competitors to travel along one side of the promenade's dual carriageway, then return by

Longridge programme, 12 May 1974.

New Brighton programme from 1964.

a similar road slightly more inland – passing several traffic islands on the 'wrong' side. It was generally agreed by the 180-strong field of competitors that the circuit with its first-class road surface was very much to their liking, helped no doubt by the unique atmosphere of the event. The winners of that initial 1960 meeting were in the 150cc Ken Martin (Ducati), 250cc Eric Cheers (196 MV), 350 and 500cc Bill Smith (AJS and Matchless) and the two sidecar events J. Bollington (Triumph).

New Brighton continued to attract a strong entry every season for the next quarter of a century and more, organised by the Wirral Hundred club.

Oulton Park

The very first motorcycle race meeting at Oulton Park, some 13 miles (21km) from Chester, took place on Saturday 3 October 1953. Situated in the grounds of Sir Phillip Grey-Egerton's estate near Tarporley, the circuit had been designed and laid down especially for racing. Measuring one and a half miles (2.4km) in length, the course was roughly rectangular in shape. It incorporated three sweeping right-handers (the track being run clockwise), a right-hand hairpin, and a shallow S-bend. The surface was tarmac and the road undulating in character. A Bailey bridge allowed spectators' vehicles to be driven on to land inside the circuit, and there was also a spectators' footbridge spanning the course at one point.

The first meeting in October 1953 was a combined Formula 3 car and motorcycle affair – although the bikes predominated in number. With a crowd in excess of 30,000, even at this inaugural meeting Oulton Park already showed signs of being an excellent circuit.

Run under a Cheshire Centre restricted permit, the motorcycle side of the event was organised by the Wirral Hundred and Mid-Cheshire clubs. The race winners that day comprised in the 250cc Maurice Cann (Moto Guzzi), 350cc Phil Carter (AJS), 500cc Denis Parkinson (Norton) and sidecars Cyril Smith (Norton).

So successful was that initial meeting and one by BMCRC a couple of weeks later, that a mere six weeks afterwards in mid-November came news that plans were going ahead to extend the circuit up to almost three miles (4.8km) in length. It was hoped that this longer course would be ready for the following spring. A typical press comment in late 1953 about Oulton and its proposed extension read, 'The racing boys approved of it mightily, as far as it goes, and the green folds of the park environment were a delightful change from the grey bleakness of disused airfields.'

The first meeting over the extended course, now 2.23 miles (3.58km), came in early May 1954 when BMCRC put on a club affair; however, the

Programme from the first meeting at Oulton Park, 3 October 1953.

Programme and map from 17 October 1953.

Programme from 2 April 1956.

Circuit map from 1958, showing the extended circuit.

extension was to be in two stages. The final length of 2.7 miles (4.35km) to be completed later that year was available for the Wirral Hundred event on 21 August that same year. It was at that latter date that the Les Graham '100' race made its debut in honour of the great rider killed the previous year in the Senior TT when he crashed the four-cylinder MV Agusta on the fearsome Bray Hill. The 23-lap event was won by George Salt (AJS), and he was presented with the beautiful Les Graham Trophy by Les's widow Edna. Over the succeeding years this award was to be won by many of racing's most legendary names.

And so to the circuit layout now that the definitive length had been reached. From the starting line (in front of the pits) riders had almost immediately to negotiate the right-hand Old Hall Corner, then they proceeded downwards (through what is now known as the Avenue) to The Cascades, a sweeping left-hander that led out onto a straight and on to the fast left-hander Island Bend, which continued to what was a super-elevated right-hand hairpin. This was known in the 1960s as Esso Bend but was later re-branded to 'Shell'. Then came the fastest point of the course (which was slowed by a chicane in the 1980s) up over a steep rise and then down to the fast, sweeping Knicker Brook section. Then came a climb up Clay Hill to Druids Corner. This double right-hander was probably the most tricky turn on the course, exiting the final part of this it was a case of full bore on the straight leading to Lodge Corner. Rounding this right-hander came a thrilling downhill exit, then rushing immediately uphill came Deer Leap, which brought riders back to the finishing straight and thus the end of the lap.

Derek Minter (Norton) leading the pack up Clay Hill, from Knicker Brook, 1967.

From 1957 the ACU Clubman's moved from the Isle of Man to Oulton but with a new format.

For the 1959 season Oulton Park took over from Thruxton as the venue for the single meeting annual British Championships. And on August Bank Holiday Monday Mike Hailwood was in scintillating form to take the 125, 250 and 500cc titles riding Ducati, FB Mondial and Norton machinery respectively.

The 1960s saw some titanic British Championship races at Oulton, with men such as Hailwood, Derek Minter, John Hartle and Bob McIntyre battling it out for the honours. Sadly, the 1962 meeting at Oulton was to see the fatal crash by McIntyre in terrible wet conditions. Also during the same decade the Wirral Hundred club's 'Racing for Sport' club meetings often attracted hundreds of novice riders and proved an ideal training ground for the stars of the future.

And so, as the decades unfolded, Oulton Park has remained one of Britain's premier circuits. It, like Brands Hatch, has seen a succession of owners including Motor Circuit Development Ltd (1964), the Foulston family (1990s), before finally, as with the other circuits within the Brands

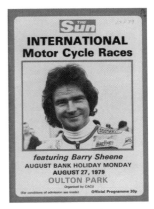

Programme cover from 27 August 1979.

Oulton Park, Transatlantic, Easter 1978. American Pat Hennen (23) and Barry Sheene (7) with their works Suzuki 500s in a star-studded field.

Heron Suzuki team members
Roger Marshall (11) and
John Newbold (5), 1981.

portfolio (Snetterton and Cadwell Park), control passed to Jonathan Palmer's Motor Sport Vision empire at the beginning of the 21st century.

During the 1970s Oulton Park (together with Brands and Mallory Park) hosted the hugely popular Transatlantic Challenge Series which saw British and American teams battling it out. The top stars from both nations took part, including John Cooper, Barry Sheene, Dave Croxford, Mick Grant, Dave Aladana, Gary Nixon, Dick Mann and Cal Rayborn.

Then, in the 1980s, the British series effectively became the *Motor Cycle News*-sponsored Superbike Championship, which together with the 125, 250, Super Sport 400 and 600cc support races became the top racing event. Today BSB (British Superbike) racing series has taken over the mantle pioneered by the *MCN* series. This is seen as the next step down from the WSB (World Superbike).

Although the grass paddock of earlier days has long since been tarmaced over and there are new, modern buildings on the site, Oulton Park, unlike some venues, has managed to retain its parkland feel with the combination of an excellent track and beautiful scenic views.

PARBOLD

The compact little circuit in the Delph Tea Gardens at Parbold, Wigan, Lancashire, held a large number of meetings during the inter-war years.

Measuring 0.85 miles (1.37km) in length, this course, which was full of twists and turns and dips, called for riding skills of the scrambles type, particularly in wet conditions. By 1932 improvements had been introduced, including, for the first time at the venue, loud speakers through which music and progress announcements could be given. Meetings that year open to North-Western Centre ACU members were held on 9 April, 7 May and 27 August. The latter was a Championship event and saw, for the first time, massed Le Mans starts – where the machines were placed on one side of the road and the riders on the other, then at the drop of the flag they would sprint to their machines.

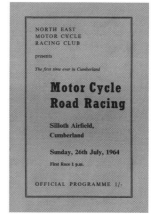

SILLOTH

Silloth Airfield on the coast of Cumbria, facing the Solway Firth between England and Scotland, was the setting for a series of race meetings over some two decades, the first of which took place on Sunday 26 July 1964. At first these were organised by the North East Motor Cycle Racing Club, but very soon the Solway Motor Cycle Racing Club took over the responsibility under its charismatic clerk of the course, Jack Horseman from Carlisle.

That first meeting in the summer of 1964 saw a crowd of 'well over 10,000' (*Motor Cycle News*) witness the Scot George Buchan dominate all solo classes except the 125cc, in which Steve Murray (Honda) led Eddie Johnson on a similar machine. Buchan led the 250 final on an Aermacchi until it blew up with a mere two laps to go, and the Padgett brothers on Yamahas took the first two places, with Buchan (Nortons) winning the 350 and 500cc races.

Programme from the opening day of motorcycle racing at Silloth.

The original track layout at Silloth.

Scot George Buchan, Norton (1), and Welshman Selwyn Griffiths, Matchless (86). Filtrate Trophy race, Silloth, April 1966.

George Buchan (1) Norton,
Bill Crossier (16) AJS, mid-
1960s.

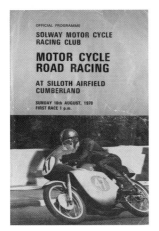

Roy Ward Mog-Vin (2) leads
conventional sidecar outfits,
mid-1960s.

1970 programme.

As for the circuit itself, this measured 1.1 miles (1.76km) and ran in a clockwise direction. The start–finish line was placed in the middle of the main straight. From there riders went on to reach the right-hand Lido Curve, followed by Hollidays Corner. This was followed by a short straight to the left–right Hanger Bends, and thereafter came a run down to the tight Hairpin and onto the main straight and thus the finishing line to complete the lap.

Due to a dispute by one of the landowners, a newer, shorter circuit was used from the 1976 season, this now running in a anticlockwise direction. The Solway club folded at the end of 1978 and no more meetings were held until 23 May 1981. This, together with all other meetings, was run by the West

Phillip Winter (350
Aermacchi), mid-1970s.

David Goodfellow (500 Suzuki-Seeley) in action at Lido Corner, Silloth, 1974.

The second, shorter Silloth course, which ran until the last meeting in 1983.

Cumbrian MCRC, until the final one was staged on 5 October 1983. The reason for Silloth's closure? Damage to the track surface by the resident cows!

THREE SISTERS

The Three Sisters circuit began life as a karting circuit. Situated at Ashton-in-Makerfield, near Wigan, Lancashire, motorcycle racing events at Three Sisters are organised by the Preston and District Motorcycle Club.

The circuit, measuring 0.8 miles (1.28km) to a lap, runs in a clockwise direction with the start and finish line in the middle of Control Straight, followed by Pentith Climb and Cowards Summit (both effectively a long curve). Next comes Joey Dunlop Corner, up to Paddock Bend and The Valley, before reaching the very tight Hairpin. The Esses and Rogersons Straight come next, before finally negotiating Lunar Bend, which leads into the Conrod Straight and thus the completion of the lap.

Although the Preston club caters for a wide range of classes, including a 501–1300cc category, it is the smaller machines to which Three Sisters is best suited. For example, at the 7 May 2007 meeting 50cc, 125cc, single cylinder and classics were all catered for, beside the more usual categories found at club events, such as Super Sport 600.

Three Sisters, circuit plan.

Teenager Alex Bedford 50cc
Minerelli, Three Sisters,
2005.

For many years Three Sisters played host to the JRA (Junior Racing Association) in which machines up to 100cc could take part with a maximum riding age of 15. This proved an important breeding ground for young British riding talent. For example, current Moto GP rider and 2004 and 2007 World Superbike Champion James Toseland began his career riding a 75cc Cagiva Prima in the JRA races at Three Sisters in 1995 – culminating in winning the JRA Championship that year.

SCOTLAND

Alford (1990)

Ballado (early 1950s)

Beveridge Park (1948–88)

Charterhall (1953–62)

Crail (1952, 1992–93)

Crimond (1951, 1955–57, mid-1960s–early 1970s)

East Fortune (1971–)

Edzell (1959, 2004)

Errol (1951–59)

Gask (1960s)

Ingliston (mid-1960s, 1979)

Kennell (1950)

Knockhill (1980s–)

Turnbury (early 1950s)

Winfield (early 1950s)

ALFORD

Within the grounds of the Grampian Transport Museum is a small (approximately a third of a mile) oval circuit. This is used for classic race demonstrations at the annual Grampian Motorcycle Convention (which celebrated its 25th anniverary in 2007), held at the beginning of September. Only one competitive motorcycle meeting was held at the venue, this taking place not long after the museum had opened, on 1 July 1990. The day included several well-known Scottish racers, including the late Jack Gow, and took the form of sprinting, rather than racing. Alford is some 20 miles (32km) west of Aberdeen.

Alford 2008 programme.

BALLADO

Ballado Airfield, Kincardine, was a typical immediate post-war makeshift race circuit created by simply using the runways and perimeter tracks from a disused wartime airfield, but this time in Scotland. In fact, the great Bob McIntyre had one of his very first road race meetings there on 23 July 1950, when riding a fellow Mercury Club member's BSA 350cc Gold Star he won three of the four races. As he recalled later, the pair simply removed the silencer and headlamp and, as Bob said, 'That was our preparation done.

Our rivals included KTT Velocettes and Manx Nortons, but I was lucky. The track was covered with loose gravel and most of the lads – all amateur riders, no great names – were nervous of the way the machines slid on it. With my scrambling experience this did not bother me and, in fact, suited me.'

BEVERIDGE PARK

Beveridge Park, Kirkcaldy, on the Fife coast had first opened way back in 1892. This was due to the sponsorship of Michael Beveridge, who had died two years earlier, leaving money in trust for the people of Kirkcaldy to create a park (and also a library and hall).

The first motorcycle race meeting, held on the perimeter road that ran just inside the park, was in the summer of 1948, the circuit measuring 1.375 miles (2.212km) in length. Motorcycles ran anti-clockwise, and the course included The Railway Dip, Raith Road, The Brae and The Snake. For the most part trees lined the narrow circuit. Another feature was the severe cambers – the road surface dropping away quite sharply from its high point in the middle of the road to assist drainage – which created something of a hazard for the riders. Another problem was moss, which was prone to form on the road surface in the areas covered by trees. In fact, this had to be 'burned off' on several occasions before racing could take place!

The first meeting was entitled The Kirkcaldy Grand Prix. In 1949 the second Scottish Road Races were run and broadcast live on BBC radio, with Graham Walker, father of Murray, doing the commentary. There were then live broadcasts from the circuit every year until 1964.

Programme 14 August 1948.

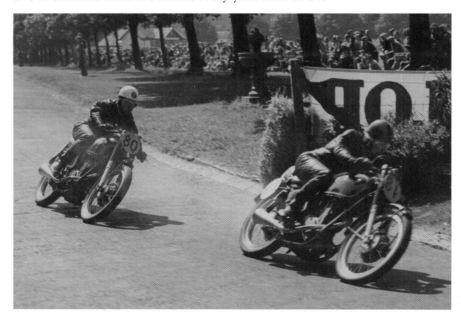

Bob McIntyre (80) trails Leslie Cooper, both AJS 7R-mounted, at Beveridge Park, c.1953.

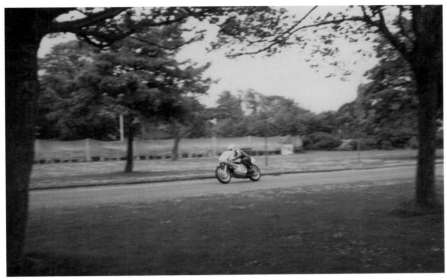

Mick Grant (350 Yamaha)
Beveridge Park, 1972.

Programme 7 May 1960.

Programme and circuit map,
22 June 1974.

During the early days of the Beveridge Park circuit not only bikes, but also cars competed (the cars racing in the opposite direction). In 1952 a combined bike/car meeting was staged.

The great Bob McIntyre made his Beveridge Park debut in 1951 and raced thereafter every year except 1954, 1956 (no meeting) and 1957, until his untimely death at Oulton Park in August 1962. He even took a works 285cc Honda four to the Fife circuit that final year. It was an act of faith to his many Scottish fans that one cannot imagine being repeated in today's big money, hi-tech MotoGP world.

Many other riders competed at Beveridge Park over the years and included Alastair King, Denis Parkinson, Bernard Hargreaves, Jimmy Buchan, Dennis Gallagher and Charlie Bruce.

Even though it was an extremely demanding course (due to not only the narrowness and awkward cambers previously described, but also the potential dangers caused by the myriad of trees) Beveridge Park continued to be a firm favourite with competitors and spectators alike. Eventually in 1988 the final meeting – billed as the 40th Scottish Road Races – was run on Saturday 18 June. The Kirkcaldy and District Motor Club were still the organisers, as they had been over the years, with the local Kirkcaldy District Council (the park owners) working together. But quite simply the latest machines had become too fast and, having walked around the circuit, I have to agree that this was the right decision.

In the context of Scottish motorcycle racing history, Beveridge Park can be truly proud of its unique role over a 40-year lifespan as a road racing venue.

Jack Gow (Norton), 1984.

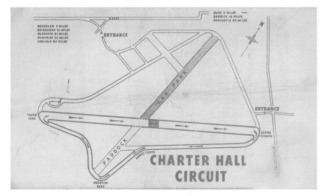

Charterhall programme and map from 1956.

Over the weekend of 5 and 6 July 2008 a special celebration of 60 years of Scottish road racing was held at the park. Although there was no actual racing it was a brilliant event, including classic and vintage motorcycle displays, trade stands, a motorcycle trial, hall of fame, custom show, dealer displays and much, much more.

CHARTERHALL

Charterhall airfield in Berwickshire replaced the Winfield circuit from the 1953 season, the two courses being some 11 miles (17.7km) apart.

Charterhall was 32 miles (51.4km) south of Edinburgh and 82 miles (132km) north of Newcastle; Duns was five miles (8.5km).

For the first few seasons, meetings were run by The Winfield Joint Committee, thereafter by the Border Motor Racing Club. On many occasions the events were for both cars and bikes.

Scotland's 'terrible twins', Bob McIntyre and Alastair King, were often the stars, but for some years there were winners from south of the border.

The circuit, measuring some 1.3 miles (2.1km) in length, ran in a clockwise direction, with the start–finish line halfway down the main straight. At the end of this straight came the hairpin-like Lodge Corner, then another, shorter straight and the left-hand Kamas Corner, followed quickly by Paddock Bend. Next came a long left sweep to the Tofts Turn, before entering the start–finish straight to complete a lap.

By the beginning of the 1960s Charterhall was running motorcycle-only meetings. In May 1961 some 400 riders took part, with classes for 125, 200, 250, 350, 500cc and sidecars. The final meeting took place there in 1962.

CRAIL

Crail, some eight miles (12.9km) south east of St Andrews on the Fife coast has had two goes at being a motorcycle racing circuit – both being organised by the Kirkcaldy and District Motor Club.

The first came in 1952 with a single meeting on Sunday 21 September over a 1.7-mile (2.73km) circuit, with riders including Alec Peetman, Alastair King, Bob McIntyre, Charlie Bruce and Bob McGregor.

The second coming of Crail was when two meetings were run by the same club in 1992 – the first on Sunday 28 June – and another two in 1993. This time the track was only one and a half miles (2.41km), due to

Kenny Moore leading the pack at Crail, Fife, 1992.

Crail programme from 1992.

problems with the landowner of the section upon which the longer part of the circuit belonged. As before, the top Scottish riders of the day competed at Crail. This time these included Jim Moodie, Ian Simpson and Alan Duffus.

In both eras the track ran in an anti-clockwise direction. Being so close to the North Sea meant that the course was very exposed to the weather.

CRIMOND

Crimond airfield, Aberdeenshire, just off the main Peterhead – Fraserburgh road, was first used as a road racing circuit on Sunday 20 May 1951. Organised by the local Aberdeen club, the circuit measured 1.8 miles (2.9km) and consisted of the main runway together with a portion of the perimeter track. The meeting attracted an entry of some 40 riders and a crowd estimated to have been approximately 16,000. There were classes for 250, 350, 500cc and Unlimited solos. The most successful rider was J. Blair (348cc AJS) who won the 350 and 500cc events and who was runner-up in the Unlimited race.

Then, some four years later, almost to the day, racing returned to Crimond in May 1955. This time there were also separate races for 350 and 500cc clubman's machines. There was another meeting at the circuit that year in late August.

In June 1956 Crimond enjoyed the presence of the legendary Bob McIntyre with a brace of Joe Potts's Nortons, in what was generally agreed to have been a record crowd of north-eastern enthusiasts. However, it was

Scottish champion George Buchan (1) pushes his Aermacchi into life at Crimond, 250cc race, May 1966.

Crimond programme and map from May 1971.

his pal Alastair King who was to clean up the larger classes with McIntyre striking mechanical trouble. The 250cc race was won by Charlie Bruce (Velocette). For the final meeting of its 1956 programme the Aberdeen club revived the old North East of Scotland Championships once held on the sands of Cruden Bay, a few miles to the south of Crimond. But it was Rae Graham (Norton), who had made the long journey from Dumfries, who established himself as the champion in both the 350 and Unlimited races.

During 1957 and 1958 the star man at Crimond was Jimmy Buchan – except when King and McIntyre made a brief return in July 1957. Then, once again, the Aberdeenshire venue disappeared from the racing calendar.

It was not until May 1966 that the Crimond again echoed to the roar of motorcycles. Unlike the majority of other circuits, Crimond seemed to alter in shape at various times, and the 1966 event was held over a shorter 1.33-mile (2.13km) course. But after a lapse of eight years this did not matter, as *Motor Cycle News* explained 'It was like the gathering of the clans at Crimond airfield in Aberdeenshire on Sunday. Thousands came from city and glen to see local champion George Buchan do battle with the Sassenach invader, John Cooper.' In the end the result was a draw, with Buchan winning the 350 and Cooper the 500cc. There were also sidecars for the first time. The programme was completed with Production 125, 200 and 250cc solos.

EAST FORTUNE

Like many other circuits the East Fortune track, about one mile (1.61km) east of Haddington in East Lothian, had its origins with a single club. In East Fortune's case this was the Edinburgh-based Melville Club, which had been in existence since 1933.

East Fortune, late 1970s. Left to right: Robbie Allan, Bill Simpson, Alan Duffus, Adam Brownlee, Tom Dickie.

The inaugural meeting was held in 1971 and was very much a 'toe-in-the-water' affair behind closed doors with no prize money, only trophies. So successful was this enterprise, however, that the club decided to put on spectator events, with cash awards from the following year. And so the first 'official' race meeting was staged at East Fortune on 23 April 1972 – this also being the first round of that year's Scottish Championships. As was fitting for such an event, the entry list included many of the country's top stars, including Alex George, John Findlay, Bob Steele, Bill Milne, John Kiddie, Bill Simpson and Alan Duffus. There were also a fair number of riders from south of the border including Crooks Suzuki teamster Les Trotter and sidecar ace Mac Hobson.

As my friend and Melville Club stalwart Dougie Muir so aptly puts it 'The Dickie clan were for many years the driving force behind race meetings at East Fortune.' This included father Tom and son Ian (the latter a solo and sidecar racer in his own right). Dougie says: 'Tom, who had worked for a large bakery in Edinburgh, was a real gentleman whose military bearing opened many doors that would otherwise have been closed to the motorcycle fraternity.'

Programme and map from 1972.

East Fortune 1972.

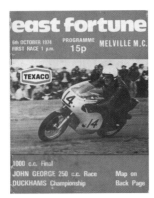

Programme from 1974.

Also playing a vital role in the history of East Fortune circuit were the landowners. Originally there were two parties for the club to contend with, but following problems, and with a slight alteration to the course, only the Pate family was left. And in succeeding years father Pete and son Alastair (Ally) Pate have proved to be true friends of the racing world.

In fact, there is even a Pate's Corner on the East Fortune circuit, so named in recognition of the family's support. The course, running in a clockwise direction (a meeting was also held early on in the opposite direction) measured 1.65 miles (2.65km). At first the start–finish was located between Railway Bend and the Esses, but it was later transformed to the current position at the other end of the pits between the Hairpin and Pate's Corner.

Perhaps the most interesting of the early East Fortune meetings came on 6 October 1974. The following is how the programme notes of the day set the scene, 'For this the last meeting in Scotland this year, we have the best entry ever seen in Scotland. It is certainly the largest, the 160-plus solo riders [actually over 170] turning out a grand total of 200 solo machines, and we also have 44 sidecar outfits. Our meetings certainly seem to be attracting riders from further afield these days. At this meeting we have 17 riders coming over from Ireland, a few from London, Inverness, the Midlands and the north of England.' And, interestingly, from a personal note, another programme extract read, 'We also have, fresh from a fine performance in the Isle of Man [runner-up by a mere couple of seconds in the Senior Manx Grand Prix] Norman Tricoglus on Mick Walker's Yamahas, in the 250 and 350 classes.'

Steve Mills and Stuart Graham, sidecar racing, 1980s.

During this period the big names at East Fortune included John Findlay and Bob Steele, the latter campaigning the 750cc Rutherford Norton tuned by Bill Crosier. Additionally, race sponsors included the Texaco Oil Company and Glasgow dealer John George (father of Alex).

Down through the years the Melville Club have continued to run a number of meetings each season, and since the late 1990s East Fortune has also become the home of the annual Bob McIntyre two-day meeting, staged each year in June, by the Scottish Classic Motorcycle Racing Club, who transferred from their original Knockhill venue from the 1999 season onwards.

Additionally, East Fortune (on the other landowner's site) runs a Sunday Market, and nearby is the internationally-known Museum of Flight which holds its annual airshow in front of vast crowds of spectators.

EDZELL

Edzell airfield, some five miles (8km) north of Brechin, Angus, was the setting for a road race meeting on 20 June 1959 which attracted a crowd of over 25,000. It was an Englishman, however, Terry Shepherd from Liverpool, who stole the thunder that day when he did the double by winning the 350 and 500cc races on his Nortons. In the big race he equalled the Formula Two car lap record of 94.7mph (152.3km/h).

Bob McIntyre anniversary programme from 2007.

Programme from 20 June 1959.

R. Lister (Norton Dominator), 7 September 1959.

Circuit map from 20 June 1959.

Programme from 23 May 2004.

1951 programme.

Errol Aerodrome, Perthshire, 26 June 1957.

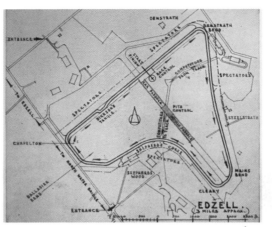

The circuit measured three miles (4.8km), and the meeting was organised by the Aberdeen and District Motor Club.

Some 45 years later the Bon Accord Motorcycle Club organised four meetings at Edzell, the first on Sunday 23 May 2004; however, this time a much shorter (approximately one mile – 1.61km), tighter circuit was used designed by Robbie Allan. Amazingly, a rider, Alastair McAllister, took part in both the 1959 and 2004 meetings!

Unfortunately, due to problems with the landowner, no more meetings were possible at Edzell from 2005 onwards.

Errol

Errol Aerodrome lay halfway between Perth and Dundee, and next to the Firth of Tay. Some two miles (3.2km) in length and in the shape of a figure eight, the course ran in a clockwise direction. Meetings at Errol were organised by the Dundee and Angus Motor Club.

Racing at Errol spanned the 1950s, from 1951 through to 1959. Certainly, at the beginning of that decade with a dirth of circuits north of the border, Errol attracted all the top Scottish road racers. For example, the entry list from Sunday 16 September 1951 included Charlie Bruce, Bob McIntyre, Alastair King, Leslie Cooper and Jock Weddell.

Although Errol could never be described as an interesting course – being very much a typical austere airfield setting – it nonetheless performed an important task of helping keep road racing alive in Scotland during the early post-war era.

By the end of the 1950s, although the entry list for meetings remained static at around the 80 mark, several new names had begun to appear such as Jack Gow, Dennis Gallagher, George Plenderlieth, Bill Crossier and Jimmy Buchan.

D. Nicoll (Velocette KTT) and Jimmy Buchan (BSA Gold Star), Errol 31 May 1954.

J. Furneaux (Furneaux Special) at Errol, late 1950s.

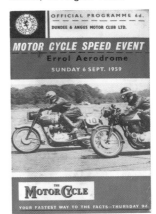

Typical Errol paddock scene, 12 August 1957.

Programme and map, 1959.

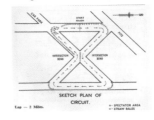

'Chappie' Chapman making adjustments to his 248cc Velocette at Errol, 12 August 1957.

E. Harris Gilbert of Kirkcaldy with his 197cc Villiers machine at Errol, 12 August 1957.

G.B. Christie (BSA Gold Star) in the Errol paddock, 18 April 1960.

Today the Errol airfield site is home to car boot sales and car auctions, plus the annual Tayside Classic Motor Show, the author attending the 2008 event, on 8 June.

GASK

Gask Airfield, near the village of Findo Gask, Clatchymore, Perthshire, was used as a motorcycle racing venue throughout most of the 1960s. During World War Two, Gask was a home for Polish fighter squadrons and was operational between 1941 and 1948. Like venues such as Errol and Crail, Gask was a stark,

147 Roy Graham (Triton) 22 June 1962 leading the field away at Gask.

open place that, on a wet, windy day, was not very friendly to either competitors or spectators. Scotland at that time was not blessed with racing circuits, however, and as such Gask at least provided a venue for the sport.

In late 1962, following Bob McIntyre's untimely death after an accident during the British Championship 500cc race at Oulton Park in August the same year, the Gask authorities attempted to put on a Bob McIntyre Memorial Meeting north of the border in this great rider's memory and to raise funds for his widow Joyce and young baby, Eleanor. Unfortunately, the fates did not conspire to assist in the weather department, resulting in the meeting having to be abandoned at the first attempt, and when it did finally take place a few weeks later poor weather restricted spectators to only a very small number.

Like certain other Scottish circuits at the time, Gask, besides the usual 250, 350 and 500cc classes, put on races for machines up to 200cc (as did Ulster meetings for many years). This often saw Dundee rider/dealer Jack Gow emerge as winner riding a 175cc Ducati.

Running in an anti-clockwise direction, the lap measured approximately one and a half miles (2.41km).

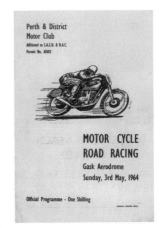

Programme, 3 May 1964.

INGLISTON

Ingliston race circuit at the Royal Highland Showground, Edinburgh, had a lap distance of 1.03 miles (1.651km). Although having hosted car events on a regular basis since the 1950s, Ingliston has a very patchy record as regards two-wheelers.

First, in 1964 came news that bikes would be catered for, but by August 1965 all further hope of racing motorcycles there had come to an end due to poor attendance figures.

Then, on 5 August 1979, the Loch Lomond Motor Cycling Club ran The Mick Grant Trophy Race Meeting. There were no less than 12 races with cash awards and 14 in total. Among the entries were riders from both north and south of the border, including Ronnie Mann, John Kiddie, Howard Selby, Bill Robertson, Dennis Gallagher, Bill Simpson and Mick Grant himself (aboard a Honda Britain 1000). But even Mick Grant's association could not light the spark for a long-term continuation of motorcycles at the Edinburgh circuit, and it soon reverted to a 'cars only' role.

Ingliston programme and circuit map from 1979.

KENNELL

Kennell, near Arbroath, Angus (also reffered to as Easthaven or Froickheim) was only used occasionally during 1950. The few events run on this disused airfield were likely to have been organised by the Dundee and Angus Club.

Programme from 1983.

Suzuki riders of the
Knockhill Racing School in
1986, in the pit lane.

KNOCKHILL

As late as the early 1970s, Scotland could still not boast a venue permanently dedicated to motor sport. A few disused airfields and the odd public park were being utilised on a part-time basis. Dependent on the goodwill of landowners or the local council, this was not an adequate solution for the modern age.

This brought Tom Kinnaird, a sheep farmer at South Lethans, Fife, into the picture. Tom was a fan of motorcycle racing and travelled regularly to meetings throughout the country. Tom's farm, in the lee of Knock Hill, some seven miles (11.26km) from Dunfermline, boasted a narrow farm service track and a disused railway line. His vision was to create a 1.3-mile (2.09km) course featuring a series of twists, turns, descents and climbs.

The gestation period was to be some two years from the initial bite of Tom's mechanical digger to laying the primary tarmac surface. Then, in the autumn of 1974 came the inaugural motorcycle race meeting at the newly opened Knockhill race circuit. Vast crowds descended upon the track, and thus Scotland's National Centre for Motor Sport was born.

Tom Kinnaird went on to operate the circuit himself for a year, offering mid-week testing facilities for both motorcycles and cars in addition to competitive weekend race meetings. But after 12 months he realised that, if Knockhill was to progress, outside resources would be needed.

The next man on the scene was Denis Dobbie. Already active with a Formula Three car team, Denis saw the potential of Knockhill and was given a one-year lease – with an option to purchase. His ultimate aim was a Scottish Formula 1 Grand Prix, but for all his ambitious plans (including an extension in track length to 2.3 miles – 3.7km), by the end of the year the project had accumulated considerable debts, and as landlord Tom Kinnaird took back the keys. Next, in conjunction with Scottish clubs (notably the Kirkcaldy and District MCC) he leased out the circuit on a year-by-year basis.

During this same period a young Derek Butcher had been taking part in motorcycle racing events, both at Knockhill and elsewhere on a variety of machines. He had also set himself up in business as Fife Alarm Services. By 1983 he had built up a considerable business. And when this business was bought out by a multinational corporation Derek Butcher decided to plough the necessary finance, together with his business acumen, into the Knockhill project on a full-time basis.

Thus Derek Butcher purchased South Lethans Farm and all its assets from Tom Kinnaird and Knockhill circuit moved up into top gear.

There was certainly a lot needing doing, and during the period since 1984 the circuit has come a long way – including being resurfaced twice and track safety being brought up to and above existing requirements. Buildings and services have been continually updated and improved, for example catering facilities now offer a first-class service, with the aptly named Kinnaird's Restaurant having a Scottish master chef in the kitchen.

The arrival of events such as British Superbikes and British Touring Car Championships during the early 1990s marked Knockhill's acceptance as a circuit on par with the leading ones south of the border. Another feature was Radio Knockhill. That service broadcast commentary on Medium Wave at every event from 1992 until 2005 and made a welcome return from the beginning of the 2007 season.

The round of the British Superbike series is the two-wheel highlight at Knockhill and until the end of the 1997 season was the responsibility of the Kirkcaldy Club. From 1998 it came under

Programme from 1989.

Programme from 1992.

The race circuit has remained pretty much unchanged since the course was opened.

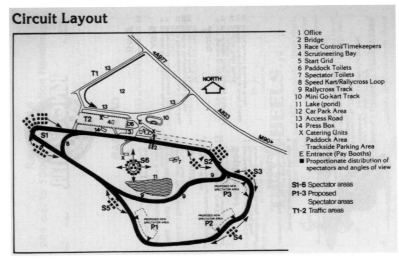

Circuit Layout

1 Office
2 Bridge
3 Race Control/Timekeepers
4 Scrutineering Bay
5 Start Grid
6 Paddock Toilets
7 Spectator Toilets
8 Speed Kart/Rallycross Loop
9 Rallycross Track
10 Mini Go-kart Track
11 Lake (pond)
12 Car Park Area
13 Access Road
14 Press Box
X Catering Units
  Paddock Area
  Trackside Parking Area
E Entrance (Pay Booths)
■ Proportionate distribution of
  spectators and angles of view

S1-6 Spectator areas
P1-3 Proposed
     Spectator areas
T1-2 Traffic areas

Programme from 2004.

Programme from 2008.

the control of the Motor Cycle Racing Control Board (who themselves had taken over the running of the series on a national (UK) basis from the ACU at the end of the 1995 season).

The Kirkcaldy Club are still very much a part of the Knockhill motorcycle racing programme, running not only rounds of the Scottish Championship but also a round of the British Sidecar series.

Although the circuit is still essentially the same length and shape as it was in the early days (always running in a clockwise direction), it has progressed in so many other ways and now fully lives up to Tom Kinnaird's original dream – that of being Scotland's National Motor Sport Centre.

TURNBURY

Turnbury, near Culzean Castle, Ayrshire, is known internationaly for its golf course. The circuit on this disused airfield was used for a few meetings in the very early 1950s. Circuit length unknown.

WINFIELD

Winfield was a typical open airfield-type circuit of the immediate post-war era and ran car and motorcycle events until it was replaced by another Berwickshire circuit, Charterhall, for the 1953 season. Certainly Charterhall is far more well known than Winfield but, in memory of the latter, the former's meetings were staged by the Winfield Joint Committee Ltd.

That legendary Scottish rider, Bob McIntyre, raced at Winfield in 1951 and 1952, the meetings on both occasions being held in April. On each occasion Bob raced the same BSA Gold Star in both the 350 and 500cc events.

WALES

Aberdare Park (1950–64, 1978–)
Anglesey (2006–)
Eppynt (1948–53)
Fairwood (1952)
Kinmel Park (early 1970s)
Llandow (late 1960s)
Mona (early 1970s)
Pembrey (early 1990s–)
Rhydymwyn (1949–early 1960s)
St Athan (1963)
Tonfanau (1993–)
Ty Croes (1992–2005)

ABERDARE PARK

The first motorcycle race meeting to be staged at Aberdare Park took place on 30 September 1950, organised by the local Aberaman Club. In 1951 came meetings on Whitsun Saturday, 12 May and 28 July.

In 1952 there were dates on 10 May and, finally, on 30 August, the first meeting to be run under a national status permit. There was certainly no lack of interest, with a record-breaking 170 entries.

1954 programme.

Keith Powell, 250cc Parvel, Aberdare Park, 1961.

Matchless G50-mounted
Selwyn Griffiths (leading
Tom Phillips), making the
fastest lap at Aberdare Park,
15 May 1963.

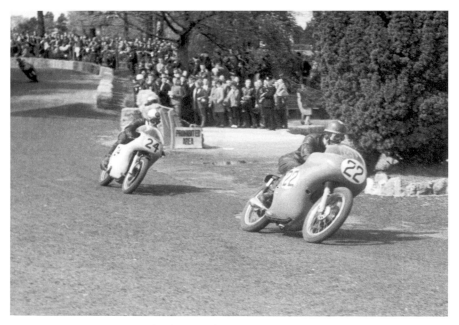

Running in an anti-clockwise direction the 0.85-mile (1.36km) circuit followed a natural road through the Welsh park. Sid Barnett, John Surtees and Len Parry were the undoubted stars of the meeting.

John Surtees well remembers his visit to the tiny welsh parkland circuit, 'Marion Pryse and her husband David, the chief organisers, extended their activities far beyond the actual running of the races. Like most other riders we were found friendly accommodation for the night in the house of one of the Aberaman Club members, and after the racing, which takes place in a park right in the centre of the town, there was a prize-giving at the circuit, high tea and a sing-song inseparable from any club activity in Wales.' During his winning ride in the 500cc event, John (on a Vincent) set a new lap record with a time of 51 seconds.

From then on until the mid-1960s Aberdare Park was to provide virtually every top-line British rider (including several world champions) the experience of racing on a tight, twisting and very testing road race circuit. These included not only John Surtees, but also Mike Hailwood (a regular visitor during his early career), Phil Read, Cecil Sandford and Bill Ivy. Hailwood described the circuit as being 'the best short circuit I have ever ridden on', going on to relate that, other than the TT, Aberdare Park was the only race meeting to give him blisters on his hands and backside from working so hard!

Bob McIntyre, the first man to ever lap the TT course at 100mph (161km/h), Dave Bennett, who rode works Nortons, and many other too numerous to mention graced the Welsh circuit. And although Barry Sheene never raced there, his father Frank most certainly did – way back in 1955! Of course, the cream of Welsh racing were often winners there, including Malcolm Uphill, the first man to lap the TT on a production roadster at over 100mph, TT winner Selwyn Griffiths and Manx Grand Prix winner Gordon Pantell. And of course another great Welshman, Ray Cowles, also rode there on many occasions.

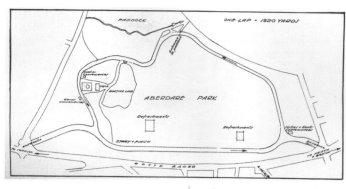

Aberdare Park was also the host for the very first 'live' outside television broadcast of a motor sport event anywhere in Great Britain, this taking place in 1955. And so after 1964 there was to be a break in racing at Aberdare Park for 14 years. Then on Saturday 24 June 1978 the Aberaman Motor Club staged the first of an annual return visit to the circuit, a tradition which remains to the present day.

Veteran Fred Launchbury was the only rider taking part who was in the previous event 14 years earlier, and the BBC cameras were there to film extracts of the meeting to show on their Sunday Sport TV programme.

Although the reborn Aberdare Park meetings have failed to attract world champions, the meetings have nonetheless proved popular with riders and spectators alike. Long may this be the case.

Circuit plan and programme from 1978.

John Creith, QUB Honda RS250, Aberdare Park, 1998.

ANGLESEY

The Ty Croes circuit had opened for motorcycles towards the end of the 1992 season and proved a popular venue because of its excellent surface and equally excellent organisation. Because of this – and the fact that both two and four wheels were catered for – plans for a much more ambitious facility were set in motion.

This was to result in the construction of the four-circuit Anglesey Motor Sport Complex near Aberfraw, which opened in 2006. Essentially the quartet of tracks are all positioned next to each other on a peninsula and are intended for international, national and club events. Part of the old Ty Croes circuit is embodied into one of the new layouts, but in a way that would not be noticeable to the casual observer.

There is no doubt that the new Anglesey complex ranks among the best in Great Britain, only its distant location working against it. It is, however, beginning to be seen as somewhere competitors would like to visit. As this book was being compiled in the spring of 2008, the CRMC (Classic Racing Motorcycle Club) had just staged a very successful meeting there which was well supported, boding well for the future of the Anglesey venue.

The full circuit length is 2.1 miles (3.37km), with shorter circuits Coastal at 1.8 miles (2.9km), National 1.2 miles (1.93km) and finally Club 0.8 miles (1.28km).

EPPYNT

Eppynt held the distinction of being the longest of the British mainland short circuits with a course measuring 5.2 miles (8.3km) in length. Situated on the Mynydd Eppynt range of mountains, near Sennybridge, Brecon, mid-Wales, meetings were staged from 1948 by permission of the War Office to which the land belonged. Not only did the Welsh circuit attract excellent entries, but with good organisation and the open country was judged to be 'perfect for spectators' (*Short Circuits!* 1950). This series of meetings was organised jointly by the Buith Wells and Carmarthen Motor Clubs. The course undulated over the contours of the mountainside – a veritable switchback to test the endurance of man and machine.

The first meeting was held on Sunday 15 August 1948 at the Royal Artillery practice camp. Its biggest problem was the inaccessible nature of the area. Only two narrow roads connected it with the outside world, and hours before the start of the meeting these roads 'carried long streams of motorcycles, coaches and cars' (*The Motor Cycle*).

The long road course ran in an anti-clockwise direction, the start line being at Dixie's Corner, 1,400 feet above sea level. There followed a straight section

Eppynt programme and circuit map, 1951.

of just over 0.5 miles (0.8km) which led into a fast left-hand bend, followed almost immediately by a right-hand swerve. The course then ran downhill into hairpin bends leading to Piccadilly Circus where it doubled back on itself in a wide left sweep. After this it climbed slightly through a cutting, with fast right and left bends, followed by a long rising straight. It then flattened out until the sharp left of Copse Corner was reached. The last section of the course included several left and right swerves, with a final rise to Dixie's Corner. In general the road was not only bumpy but quite narrow, while the surface was tar-bound chippings. In some parts of the track these chippings were loose, and riders soon found it an advantage to have a flexible engine. Because of this, lap speeds were somewhat slower than anticipated.

The 1948 meeting attracted many top riders, including Maurice Cann, George Brown, Les Graham and a very young Cecil Sandford having one of his first-ever races on Arthur Taylor's MOV Velocette; Bob Foster was a notable non-starter. Race distances were of note, with the 350cc event being over 10 laps (52 miles/83.6km) and the Unlimited being 15 laps (78 miles/125.5km). It was an unfamiliar name, J.D. Daniels, riding a 348cc Velocette who emerged victorious in the Unlimited race and who also finished runner-up (behind Les Graham, AJS) in the 350cc event.

The second meeting was held on Saturday 15 May 1949 and saw Sid Barnett (498cc Triumph) set a new course lap record of exactly 70mph (112.6km/h), while finishing runner-up to Les Graham (AJS) in the main race the Unlimited event. Graham also repeated his victory in the 350cc class.

Les Archer Jnr (348cc Velocette), in action at Eppynt, 14 May 1949.

Eppynt, 1952. The start of
the 350cc race – not a
motorhome in sight!

A third meeting was staged on 6 May 1950, with over 30,000 spectators present and Les Graham again being victorious in both the 350 and Unlimited races – on the same 348cc AJS 7R he had ridden the previous year. But it was again that man Barnett (now riding a 499cc Norton) who broke the lap record at 70.65mph (113.67km/h).

A feature of the 1951 meeting was the debut at the Welsh road circuit of Dickie Dale (Norton), who won both the Junior and Senior events and who in the Junior (350cc) raised the lap record to 71.12mph (114.43km/h).

While superb weather conditions had been a feature of previous Eppynt meetings, the 1952 event (again held in May) was just the reverse, and conditions were unpleasant indeed with heavy rain throughout. Sid Barnett at last gained victory (in the Senior race) and, incredibly considering the conditions, managed to put in a fastest lap of just over 70mph (112.6km/h).

It was back to sunny conditions a year later at the beginning of May 1953 when Sid Barnett (348cc Norton) smashed lap records in the Junior and Senior events. Having broken lap records at Eppynt in previous years, Barnett proceeded to demolish Dale's 1951 record of 71.12mph (114.43km/h) with a lap speed of 72.11mph (116.02km/h) in the Senior race. Cecil Sandford (Velocette) won both the Lightweight and Junior events, the latter after Barnett had crashed out.

In March 1954 it was announced that during an inspection of the circuit it was considered that the roads had deteriorated seriously during the winter and were not in satisfactory condition for high-speed racing. This popular and unique venue, therefore, came to a premature end.

350cc race winner Denis Parkinson (Manx Norton) taking the flag at Fairwood, 24 July 1954.

FAIRWOOD

Fairwood Aerodrome was the setting for a combined motorcycle and car meeting on Saturday 26 July 1952. A full programme was divided between two and four wheels. The best lap put up by a 500cc motorcycle of over 72mph (115.8km/h) was by H.L. Williams (Norton), a speed exactly the same as the best 500cc car.

The Fairwood circuit, near Swansea, measured 1.17 miles (1.88km) in length. It consisted of a long, fast runway straight, a fairly sharp 180-degree turn, another fast straight along a section of the perimeter track, and a return to the runway straight through another 180-degree bend. The two straights thus ran parallel and were situated very close together. The surface was generally good, but the runway had a pronounced undulation around the halfway mark.

Interestingly, a certain Australian, K. Campbell, riding a 348cc Velocette KTT, was the winner of the 350cc class and runner-up on the same bike in the 500cc. This was the very same Keith Campbell who, riding for the Italian Moto Guzzi team, would win the 350cc World Championship in 1957.

KINMEL PARK

Kinmel Park in North Wales, a couple of miles west from the holiday resort of Rhyl, was an army camp used for training military drivers. Some 0.75 miles (1.2km) in length, the track had a concrete surface. It was used by the Wirral Hundred club in the early 1970s. The track was little wider than an

Fred Pidcock (14) on the ex-
Angelo Bergamonti; 402cc
Aermacchi, Kimnel Park, 24
March 1973.

Programme and circuit plan
and from 1965.

army lorry in most places, and the surface was loose. Solo machines were limited to eight, while sidecars were started off individually on a timed basis.

The camp, which was operational when used for racing, had a very sad history. It had been there, on 4–5 March 1919, that a mutiny took place among the Canadian soldiers stationed there. Still awaiting repatriation long after World War One they were billeted in awful conditions over the winter which culminated in riots, during which five men were killed and 23 wounded. Seventy-eight others were arrested, of whom 23 were formally convicted of mutiny.

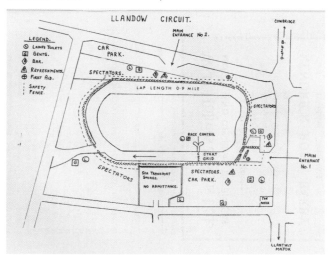

LLANDOW

In spring 1965 it was announced that, although Aberdare Park had sadly been lost for roadracing (a situation that was to continue for some 14 years until, eventually, it made a comeback at the parkland circuit), a new course had been found in South Wales. This was Llandow airfield, near Cowbridge, and the Barry Motor Club had fixed two dates for meetings there on 15 May and 24 July that year.

The first of these two meetings attracted 125 solos and 23 sidecars, with a programme of 24 races (heats and finals) including a number of top racing men, such as Selwyn Griffiths, Malcolm Uphill, Billie Nelson, Ron Pladdys, Robin Good and Louis Carr. It was Uphill who won the 350, 500 and Unlimited finals, with Ron Pladdys victorious in the smaller classes. And it was Griffiths again who repeated the exact performance in the July meeting.

The circuit, owned by the South Wales Auto Club and measuring 0.9 miles (1.44km), was saved from simply being rectangular by an elbow known as 'Devil's.'

Although meetings continued for some years at Llandow, the extremely bumpy nature of the circuit did not endear itself to the competitors and so entries suffered in due course.

MONA

Mona Airfield in Anglesey, North Wales, saw racing take place there during the early 1970s courtesy of the Cheshire Motor Cycle Road Racing Club. Their race programme for Saturday 1 July 1972 made the following acknowledgement, '[the club] wish to express their thanks to Squadron Leader Stark and the RAF for the use of the Aerodrome and the volunteers who have helped make the day a success. Without these people who come along to give their valuable time for the "love of the sport" there would be no racing at all.'

Programme from 1972.

Fred Pidcock (AJS 7R), Mona, Anglesey, 22 April 1972.

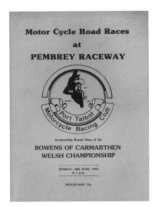

Programme and circuit map,
1985.

Pembrey programme, 1994.

Pembrey, Super Sport 400
race, summer 1993.
Paddock Bend.

That day there were a total of 23 races for solos and sidecars, including heats and finals. Riders included Nev Watts (182cc Honda), Vic Sousson (Yamaha), Pete Welfare (Honda) and Derek Huxley (Yamaha). This surely was what racing at club level was all about – an excellent day's sport and genuine enthusiasm by riders, spectators and organisers.

PEMBREY

Like Thruxton and Mallory Park, Pembrey, located a couple of miles west of Burry Port on the South Wales coast, is currently owned by the BARC (British Automobile Racing Club). With the official title of the Welsh Motor Sports Centre, Pembrey first received official approval to run race meetings back in May 1989. Besides motorcycle racing, the Pembrey facilities have also been used for car testing and rallycross.

The circuit runs in a clockwise direction and measures 1.456 miles (2.342km) in length. The start line is in the middle of Park Straight, and riders have to apply the brakes hard to negotiate Hatchets Hairpin. This is quickly followed by the Spitfire complex, which in turn is followed by the left-hand Dibeni Bend. Next there is the Esses and then the right-hand Brooklands Hairpin. After this comes the quickest section of the course, embracing Speedway Straight, Woodlands and finally Honda Curve before speeding down Park Straight to complete the lap.

Several clubs run meetings at Pembrey, notably New Era MCC and the CRMC (Classic Racing Motorcycle Club). During the mid-1990s Pembrey hosted a round of the national Supercup series, the forerunner of today's BSB (British Superbike) Championships, but Pembrey was not included when the new series took over.

Rhydymwyn

The first meeting at Rhydymwyn, near Mold in North Wales, took place on Saturday 25 June 1949 and was organised by the Wirral Hundred Motor Club (as were all subsequent events). The 0.5-mile (0.8km) circuit was just off the main Denbigh-Mold road. Running in an anti-clockwise direction, the start line was next to the pits. First came Railway Straight, followed by Coppice Bend, The Esses, Wood Straight, Mold Straight and finally Gwysanay Straight. The surface was of concrete, and the fastest lap speeds were in the region of 42mph (67.5km/h). Interestingly, this first meeting began at 4pm and ended at 9pm. According to the organisers these times had been chosen 'so that those not blessed with a five-day working week could still attend.'

Another meeting was held later that year and saw Fron Purslow emerge as the top man, riding BSAs in all classes and winning three of them (150, 250 and 500cc). The existing course record was broken three times during the day. Purslow continued to be a race winner at Rhydymwyn for several years, riding a variety of machines. For example on 23 June 1956 he even rode a Britax Hurricane in the 50cc race, the little Britax actually being powered by a 49cc Ducati engine.

As the years rolled by, the Wirral Hundred Club continued to hold two or three meetings annually over the tight little North Wales track, even though by now it was also running meetings at Oulton Park. The club also staged car sprints on part of the course.

At the 23 September 1961 meeting there was an entry of 141 solos and 16 sidecars. Competitors included Mick Manley (220 Ducati and 348 Norton), Ivor Watton (125, 175 and 250 Ducati and 500 Triumph), Ron Pladdys (175 Ducati and 250 NSU), Chris Conn (500 Norton), Keith Heckles (350 BSA) and local champion Eric Cheers (350 and 500 BSA).

As one commentator put it that year, 'If it is value for money you want then you are hardly likely to beat Rhydymwyn, which provides over four hours of continuous racing for half-a-crown. You will not find the Hartles and Hailwoods there, but you'll have enough excitement and incident to last the rest of the week.'

St Athan

Organised by the Barry Motor Club, a single meeting was staged at RAF station St Athan, near Cardiff, on Saturday 17 August 1963. St Athan was at the time a training establishment which had a quiet time during August each year.

The Barry Club were fortunate to enlist the interest of the station commander, Air Commodore J.W. Bayley, who gave every possible help that

Programme cover, 1955.

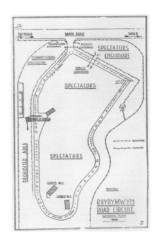

Circuit plan, 1960.

Programme from the first
meeting at Tonfanau, 1993.

Programme and Tonfanau
circuit map, 2007.

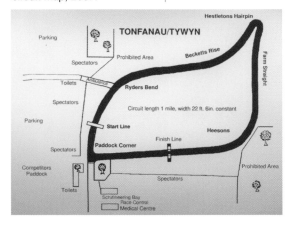

the station could provide – equipment, medical services, ambulances, public address systems and even RAF personnel.

The course was a D-shape of almost two miles (3.2km) in length, which had already been test ridden by Selwyn Griffiths. St Athan certainly attracted several top riders, including John Cooper, Tom Phillips and Chris Conn, while sidecars were seen for the first time in South Wales since the Eppynt races of the 1950s with an entry which included Bill Boddice. The winners of the finals were, in the 125cc Dave Simmonds (Tohatsu), 250cc Tom Phillips (Greeves), 350, 500 and Unlimited John Cooper (Nortons), while the sidecar event was P.H. Horton (Triumph).

Unfortunately, service commitments meant that St Athan was only used the once.

TONFANAU

The first meeting to be held at Tonfanau, some two miles (3.2km) north of Tywyn on the mid-Wales coast, was held on Sunday 11 April 1993 and organised by the Crewe & Nantwich Road Racing Combine.

Just how this came about is an interesting story in itself. The previous September, former 125cc British champion Lee Heeson came back from holiday and told fellow members of the Crewe and South Cheshire Motor Club that he had found a venue for a race circuit some 100 miles (161km) from home. At first they thought he was mad, but after numerous weekends spent working there together with colleagues from the Nantwich and District Motor Club and a few enthusiastic locals, often in adverse weather conditions, the circuit was finally finished.

At that first meeting there were a total of 21 races, classes being single cylinder 100–250cc, 240–440cc, 450–1100cc, classic machines, and Formula Two sidecars, with heats and finals where necessary.

As for the circuit itself, this measured one mile (1.61km) and the start and finish lines were in different locations. From the former, riders took the sweeping right-hander of Ryders Bend and then the equally fast left-hand Becketts Rise to Hesletons Hairpin. Then came Farm Straight, followed by the fast Heeson right-hand curve which then brought riders back to the finish line. This was followed by the sharp right Paddock Corner and soon afterwards the start line. The absolute lap record (established on 9 July 2006) is jointly held by Martin Powell, Tim Poole and Jay Bellers-Smith.

TY CROES

The first meeting at Ty Croes took place on 11 October 1992, with Tim Poole (Honda) setting the fastest lap in the 600 Supersport race. Other classes were 125, 350, 1300cc plus 400 Supersport and two other classic races – one for up to 350cc, the other over 350cc.

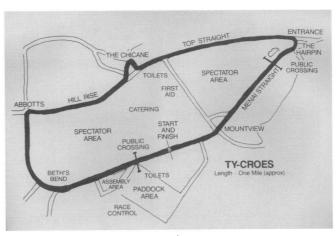

Ty Croes circuit plan and programme, 1993.

The circuit length was one mile (1.6km). The shape was very much like Mallory Park before the Leicestershire track was altered; there was even a Hairpin. Other sections included the Menai Straight, Beth's Bend, Abbotts, Hill Rise, The Chicane and Top Straight.

Besides the motorcycle races (organised by the Wirral Hundred Club), Ty Croes also hosted various car rally events (mostly in the form of stages), plus rounds of the British Rallycross Drivers Association National Rallycross Championships.

Ty Croes was absorbed into the extended three-circuit Anglesey Motor Sport Complex, which opened in 2006.

ISLE OF MAN

Andreas (1951, 1969–early 1970s)
Jurby (1970–)
Manx Grand Prix (1923–)
Southern 100 (1955–)
Tourist Trophy:
> Short Circuit (1907–10)
> Mountain Circuit (1911–)
> Clypse Circuit (1954–59)
> Southern Circuit (2008)

Note:
As with Northern Ireland (Chapter 9), both short circuits and event names are employed for the Isle of Man.

Andreas
The former World War Two fighter airfield at Andreas was first used, briefly, for racing in the early 1950s. A little-remembered fact is that in 1951 a then unknown Rhodesian (now Zimbabwe) Ray Amm took part in an Andreas meeting that summer.

In December 1968 the chairman of the Andreas Racing Association, Wilf Halsall, revealed that it was planned that two meetings would be staged in 1969 on the proposed three-mile (4.8km) circuit in the north of the island. Things did not go according to plan, however, resulting in a move in the early 1970s to Jurby airfield.

Jurby

Programme, 4 June 1977.

Jurby airfield had long been used for the testing of TT and Manx GP riders' machinery. However, the Andreas Racing Association (so-named from the circuit used during the immediate post-war era) had run meetings from the early 1970s. Up to 1976 all these had been closed-to-club, helping local riders qualify for a National competition licence, but this was not enough to be accepted for the Manx Grand Prix. For this purpose the club ran its first national status meeting on Saturday 4 June 1976, which proved a big success. Every lap and race record was broken, including the 100mph (161km/h) barrier. This was achieved by Welshman Gordon Pantell who lapped at 103.476mph (166.492km/h).

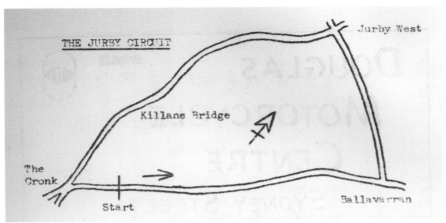

The Jurby road circuit plan, 1977.

Programme, 29 May 1976.

The Jurby road circuit, measuring 4.4 miles (7.1km), was an undulating tarmacadam surface and ran from Ballaugh Cronk, along Ballamone Moar straight via the Ballavarran Road to Jurby West and back to Ballaugh Cronk. Besides the road circuit is the airfield short circuit, with several configurations.

MANX GRAND PRIX

The Manx Motorcycle Club was formed in 1912 and provided enthusiasts in the Isle of Man with various motorcycle sports, but it is for the Manx Grand Prix that the club has received worldwide fame.

In 1923 the committee, headed by Canon E.H. Stenning decided to put on amateur races for riders to compete over the 37.73-mile (60.70km) Tourist Trophy (TT) Mountain Circuit.

From 1923 until 1927, the races were known as the Manx Amateur Motor Cycle Road Races. The first such event was staged on 20 September 1923 and in that first year, and indeed until 1929, there was just one class, 500cc, with a special award for a 350cc machine. Councillor A.B. Crookhall, the mayor of Douglas, presented the club with its main trophy, while *The Motor Cycle* donated a trophy for best three-fifty. The race took in five-laps, covering 188.65 miles (303.53km); the winner was Len Randles (Sunbeam), who averaged 52.77mph (84.90km/h). Second place went to Ken Twemlow (New Imperial) who also won the 350cc event.

In 1928, for the first time in the Manx there was a separate race for 350s which was won by Harry Meagan (Rex Acme), while Tim Hunt (Norton) won the Senior with a record breaking average speed of 67.94mph (109.31km/h) for the six-lap race.

The birth of the Manx Grand Prix was in 1930. This was marked by the victories of Doug Pirie (Velocette) in the Junior and Ralph Merrill (Rudge) in the Senior.

1948 advert.

Manx Grand Prix practice
week, 1949. Derby Square
stables, Douglas: R. Rodgers,
F. Norris, R.E. Geeson,
E.V.C. Hardy.

The decade saw many famous names take part, including Harold Daniell,
Austin Munks, Freddie Frith, Bob Foster, Denis Parkinson, Maurice Cann
and Johnny Lockett to name but a few.

1938 was the final series before World War Two. By now there were three
classes: the Lightweight (250cc), Junior and Senior, won respectively by
Parkinson (Excelsior) and Ken Bills (Nortons) in the two latter classes.

The 1946 Manx Grand Prix races were the first to be held on the TT
course after the conflict, Irishman Ernie Lyons winning a rain-soaked Senior
with the prototype Grand Prix Triumph.

The 1949 meeting saw the Lightweight race deleted from the programme,
with victories in the Junior by Cromie McCandless and Senior Geoff Duke, both
Norton mounted. In 1952, Bob McIntyre made his Manx GP debut, winning
the Junior and finishing the Senior in second on the same 348cc AJS 7R.

Yet more future stars passed through the Manx 'academy' during the
remainder of the 1950s, including John Hartle, Geoff Tanner, Jimmy
Buchan, Bob Anderson and Alan Shepherd, while Phil Read (Norton) won
the 1960 Senior.

A rider negotiating Quarter Bridge during the 1959 Manx Grand Prix.

For 1962 there were a number of rule changes, the main one being that streamlining was now allowed for the first time. In 1964 the Lightweight made a return with victory going to Gordon Keith (Greeves).

Then, almost a decade later, in the 1973 Junior, Phil Haslam (Yamaha) not only won the race, but lapped at 103.15mph (166km/h) – the first-ever 100mph Manx GP lap.

And so the Manx Grand Prix progressed into the modern era. In the 21st century there are events for both modern racing machines and classics. It remains popular with riders and spectators alike. For information on the circuit itself, readers are advised to consult the section dealing with the TT Mountain circuit.

SOUTHERN 100

The first Southern 100 road race meeting was staged on Thursday 14 July 1955. Thousands of holidaymakers watched exciting racing over the 4.25-mile (6.83km) Billown circuit, which was situated on the outskirts of Castletown, Port St Mary and Port Erin, in the south of the island.

From the start and finish, running in a clockwise direction, the course went to the first of four sharp right-hand hairpin-type bends at Ballakeighan. Then proceeding out into the country taking in Iron Gate and Ballaorris to the next hairpin Ballabeg. Then came another fast stretch including Ballwhetstone, Willows Corner and Billown Dip, to the Cross Fourways hairpin. The next landmark was Church Bends, followed by

1958 Isle of Man Southern 100 Programme.

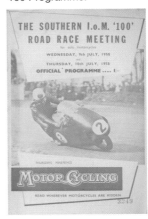

Great Meadow and finally Stadium Bend, before reaching the final hairpin Castletown Corner. It was then a case of blasting up to the start line to complete the lap.

The Southern 100 was organised by the Southern MCC, and it was their first venture into road racing as opposed to short circuit events, having previously staged the latter at the disused airfield at Andreas.

The first winner of the main (500cc) race, held over 24 laps (100 miles – 161km), was Norton-mounted Terry Shepherd, who also recorded the fastest lap of the day at 80.95mph (130.24km/h). Other race winners at that first-ever meeting were, in the 250cc Dave Chadwick (Reg Deardon Special) and 350cc Derek Ennett (AJS).

In 1956 the meeting was an even bigger success, with a star-studded field and the maximum number of entries in both the 350 and 500cc races. But again Terry Shepherd was victorious in the 500cc event, with Bob McIntyre taking the 350cc and Bill Smith the 250cc.

In 1959 McIntyre raised the lap record to precisely 85mph (136.7km/h). And this record remained until Phil Read (Norton) put it up to 87.03mph

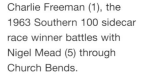

Charlie Freeman (1), the 1963 Southern 100 sidecar race winner battles with Nigel Mead (5) through Church Bends.

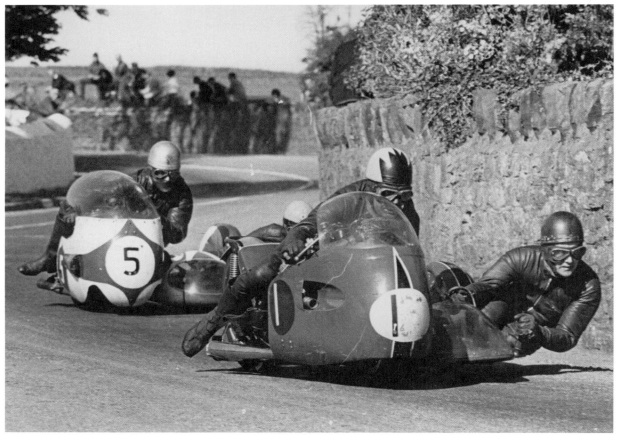

(140km/h) in 1961. The following year saw sidecars take part for the first time, joining the 125cc which had been welcomed the previous season. Read's record stood until 1971, when Yamaha-mounted K. Daniels equalled his speed. Finally, in 1972 Charlie Williams on another Yamaha raised it to 88.43mph (142.28km/h).

The first 90mph (145km/h) lap – actually 91.2mph (146.74km/h) – was achieved in 1975 by Irishman Ray McCulloch (348cc Yamaha).

In 1967 John Patrick became the first and only man to have won the Southern 100 on both two and three wheels after victory in the sidecar race, adding to his victory in the 250cc event in 1960.

1963 circuit map and programme.

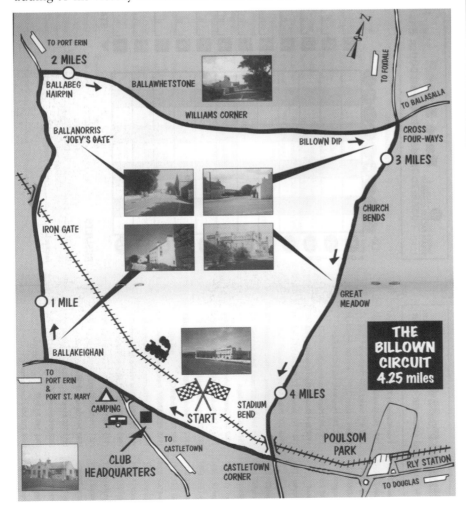

2005 programme.

The Billown circuit as it is now. Little has changed from years ago.

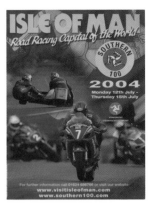

2004 programme.

From 1969 a large number of annually awarded trophies and cups were presented, including the Ennett Memorial award.

The Southern 100 has gone on from strength to strength, and by 2004 it could boast four action-packed days of competition with sponsorship from the Steam Packet Company. The racing was followed by the unique open air presentation in Castletown Square, adding a special finale to what has become known as 'the friendly races.'

TOURIST TROPHY

The TT (Tourist Trophy) began on the morning of Tuesday 28 May 1907, when 17 singles and eight twins paraded at St John's to have their petrol measured out. Class one bikes (singles) were allowed one gallon (four and a half litres) for every 90 miles (144.8km), and the twins could have one for every 75 (120.7). They had to cover 10 laps of the 15.8-mile (25.4km) course and machines started in pairs every minute. Pedalling gear was permitted! Charlie Collier (Matchless) and Rem Fowler (Peugeot-Norton) won the singles and twin events respectively.

The Short Circuit

This first course started and finished in St John's by the Tynwald Hill. The route ran anti-clockwise to Ballacraine, along the present course by Glen Helen, up Creg Willey's Hill to Kirkmichael, where it U-turned left, following the coast road via the awkward Devil's Elbow, to Peel and back to St John's. This was known as the Short Course.

The two-class system was abandoned in 1909 in favour of a straight race for singles up to 500cc and multis up to 750cc. At the same time fuel restrictions were abandoned. In 1910 H.H. Bowen (BAT twin) put up the fastest-ever lap of the Short Circuit – 53.15mph (85.51km/h).

The following year, 1911, the TT moved to the Mountain Course of 37 miles and four furlongs, while Junior and Senior classes were introduced for the first time.

In 1914 the start–finish line moved to the top of Bray Hill. Safety helmets and tyre security bolts were made compulsory, while *The Motor Cycle* proposed a 250cc class and put up a trophy.

Then came the war, and racing did not resume until 1920. The following year for the first and only time, the Senior was won by a 350cc, Howard Davies winning the race on the same AJS he had used to finish runner-up in the Junior. Then, in 1923 the first Sidecar TT race was staged, and in 1925 Walter Handley (Rex Acme) became the first man to win two TTs in a week.

The 1935 Lightweight (250cc) TT saw the first win on a foreign bike since 1911, when an American Indian had won the newly introduced Senior. The 1935 rider was Irishman Stanley Woods and the machine an Italian Moto Guzzi; Woods also won the Senior on a Guzzi v-twin.

In 1937, Freddie Frith put the Senior lap record above 90mph (144.8km/h) for the first time, riding a works Norton. The following year Harold Daniell upped the record to over 91mph (146.4km/h), a record that was to stand for 12 years.

On the very eve of World War Two, Georg Meier took the Senior trophy back to Germany after winning the blue riband event on a BMW. Post-war, the TT returned in 1947 – without supercharging – and with pool petrol. Norton took the Senior, Velocette the Junior.

The 1950 event aw the arrival of the McCandless Featherbed Norton, and with it the Birmingham factory took the first three places in both the Senior and Junior races.

In 1957, the Golden Jubilee of the TT, the Scot Bob McIntyre won both the Junior and Senior races on four cylinder Gileras and also became the first man in TT history to lap the Mountain Course at over 100mph (161km/h).

Artie Bell (Norton), Senior TT winner at 84.97mph in the 1948 event, receiving the finishing flag.

TT programme from 1949.

Dario Ambrosini, seen here at Kirkmichael village, during the 1950 Lightweight TT, which he won at record speed. The photograph captures fully an era long since gone of unfaired machines, black leathers, 'pudding basin' helmet and totally unrestricted spectator access.

Two years later, in 1959, came the first appearance of Japanese machines, when the Honda factory won the 125cc team prize and in 1960 Derek Minter (Norton) set the first 100mph-plus lap on a single cylinder machine.

The new decade also witnessed a titanic battle for supremacy between Honda, Suzuki and Yamaha. Even so, MV Agusta still reigned supreme in the Senior (500cc) class, with Giacomo Agostini taking over where Mike Hailwood had been; however, the Japanese – now with Hailwood in their ranks – proved unbeatable in the other solo classes.

1966 saw the racing postponed until August, due to the seaman's strike.

However, in 1967 the Diamond Jubilee TT was held, and Hailwood showed the true mark of a champion when he not only became 250 and 350cc World Champion, but also won the 250, 350 and 500cc TTs on Honda machinery.

Following the death of the Italian Gilberto Parlotti in the 1971 125cc TT, many top-liners, including Giacomo Agostini and Phil Read, refused to ride there. Subsequently, over the next two decades the TT declined, at least

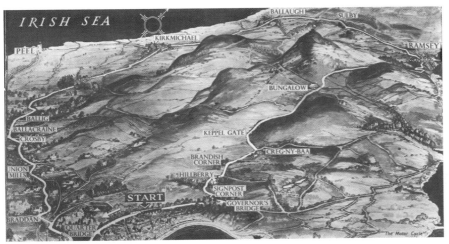

1950s map of the TT Mountain course.

1955 advert.

compared to its former status. This was, of course, except for Hailwood's magic 1978 comeback, when he rode a Ducati v-twin to a famous victory.

But even so, to many the TT remains a very special event, and in June 2007 it celebrated its centenary.

The Mountain Circuit

First used in 1911, the 37.73-mile (60.70km) Mountain Circuit is, to many, what the TT is all about.

The start, grandstand, scoreboard and pits are situated in Glencrutchery Road, high above the town of Douglas. Soon after leaving there is the slight

The Clypse circuit, Australian Bob Brown (9) leads 18-year-old Mike Hailwood (18). Both riders are mounted on NSU Sportmax machines, in the 1958 250 TT, Hailwood finished third, Brown fourth.

Cover of a 1960s TT course map.

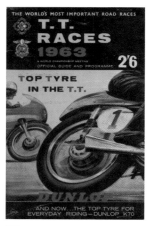

TT programme from 1963.

World Champion Mike Hailwood winning the 1964 Senior TT aboard his works 500cc four-cylinder MV Agusta.

Tarquinio Provini (Benelli four) 1964 Lightweight TT, rounding Quarter Bridge.

rise of Brown's Hill, followed by the drop to Quarter Bridge, a slow right-hander needing hard braking, engagement of bottom gear and usually the use of the clutch. Bradden Bridge is the next landmark, a spectacular S-bend over the railway and river, then on to the Union Mills three miles from the start. Winding and undulating, the course drops down to the Highlander and through the bends at Greeba to Ballacraine (7.25 miles) – a sharp right-hander.

The course is now very much out in the country, with the road twisting and turning through the leafy tunnel of the Neb Valley, past Laurel Bank and Glen Helen, then up the 1:10 rise of Creg Willey's Hill to the heights of Cronk-y-Voddee. The descent of Baaregarroo before the 13th Milestone section is generally seen as the quickest part of the course. It is followed by a tricky section ending with Westwood's Corner, a relatively fast left-hander.

Soon riders reach Kirkmichael (14.5 miles), with its second gear right-hander, followed by a trip through the narrow village street, after which there is a winding but fast stretch to Ballaugh – with the famous humpback bridge where both wheels leave the ground. Left, right, left – the trio of Quarry Bends is taken in the region of 100mph or more, the bends leading on to the start of the famous mile-long Sulby Straight, with, at its end, an extremely sharp right-hand corner on Sulby Bridge (20 miles). Then comes hard acceleration up to and around the long sweeping left-hander at Ginger Hall. Through wooded Kerromoar and the foot of Glen Auldyn, the circuit winds its way on to the town of Ramsey, where riders flick right-left through Parliament Square in the very heart of the town. Then comes the beginning

Typical TT racng. A 1970s shot showing some of the hazards of this road circuit.

1969 Junior TT, Roy Graham (Drixton-Aermacchi).

of the long mountain climb, the road rising up May Hill to the testing Ramsey Hairpin (24.5 miles) and up again to Waterworks Corner and the Gooseneck.

Still climbing, riders pass the Guthrie Memorial and reach East Mountain Gate (28.5 miles), where the long, gruelling ascent at last begins to flatten out. A further mile on leads to a quartet of gentle bends at the Verandah section, followed by the bumpy crossing of the mountain tracks at the Bungalow. The highest point on the course is at Brandywell, a left-hand sweep beyond the Bungalow, and from there the road begins to fall gently, through the aptly-named Windy Corner, a medium fast right-hander and the long 33rd Milestone Bend.

Kate's Cottage (around 0.2 miles past Keppal Gate) marks the beginning of the flat out, exhilarating sweep down to Creg-ny-Baa (34.5 miles). Still

Percy Tait, Yamaha TZ750,
during the 1977 TT, entering
Ramsey.

Keith Martin 500cc class
winner of the 1974
Production TT on his three-
cylinder Kawasaki two-
stroke.

Mick Grant (18) and Graeme
Crosby (Suzukis) battle it
out in the 1981 TT, on the
final lap, at the Nook.

Chas Mortimer (15) and Takazumi Katayama at the start of the 1978 Senior TT, both on Yamahas.

dropping, the course sweeps towards the left-hand Brandish Corner and down yet more to the fast right-hander at Hillberry.

With less than two miles to the finish, there follows the short climb of Creg-ny-Mona and the sharp right-hand turn at Signpost Corner. Bedstead Corner and The Nook follow in swift succession, and within a quarter of a mile it is a case of hard on the brakes for Governor's Bridge – an acute hairpin – which is the slowest corner on the course. The short detour through the hollow was a link to earlier days when it formed part of the main road. Once out of the hollow, riders accelerate into Glencrutchery Road less than half a mile from the grandstand and pit area.

View of the island, c.1983

Joey Dunlop (Honda),
1984 TT.

In essence, the course remains the same as years gone by, but there is no doubt that it is considerably faster, thanks to improvements which have seen the surface much smoother.

The Clypse Circuit
Used from 1954 until 1959, the Clypse Circuit hosted the 125, 250cc and sidecar events. Like the Mountain Circuit, the Clypse course – measuring

1986 Production TT, Danny Shimmin (Suzuki RG500).

10.79 miles (17.36km) – placed great emphasis on rider ability. The start and finish were still in Glencrutchery Road. The circuit then led to the top of Bray Hill, where the road turned sharp right, through Parkfield Corner and so on to Willaston Corner. Willaston was followed by Edges One and Edges Two, bends which called for extreme caution. At Cronk-ny-Mona, 1.75 miles from the start, the Mountain Course was joined, and followed in the reverse direction through Hillberry (2.25 miles) and Brandish Corner (2.75 miles) to Creg-ny-Baa (3.75 miles). The road then turned right, leaving the Mountain Course, and dropped down through Ballacarrooin (4.75 miles) to Ballacoar Corner (five and a half miles), a tight right-hand hairpin. The circuit then wound its way on for the next 2.75 miles to Morney Four Corner, where it joined the main Onchan-Laxey road. The course from then on was fast all the way to Onchan, where it turned sharp right at the Manx Arms (nine and a half miles). Then the road climbed through Nursery Bends to the acute left-hand turn at Signpost corner (10 and a half miles). The Mountain Circuit was then rejoined and followed through Bedstead Corner, The Nook, Governor's Bridge (where the loop was by-passed) and on to the Glencrutchery road and the finish line.

Southern Circuit

In June 2008 the 125 and 250cc TTs were run over the Southern 100 (Billown) course, making four Tourist Trophy circuits. Information on this circuit can be found under the Southern 100 heading in this chapter.

NORTHERN IRELAND

Aghadowey (1975–2007)

Aldergrove Airfield (1946–47)

Ballydrain (1922)

Ballykelly Airfield (2008–)

Ballynahinch (1921–25, 1927–29)

Banbridge – Bann 50 (1921)

Banbridge 100 (1928–30)

Bangor Castle (1945–50, 1966)

Bishopcourt (1968–72, 1992–)

Bush – Dungannon Revival Meeting (2006–)

Carrowdore 100 (1925–36, 1952–2000)

Clandeboye (1922)

Coleraine 100 (1923)

Comber (1937–38)

Cookstown 100 (1922–)

Desertmartin (1921)

Dundrod 100 (1950–51)

Dundrod 150 (1993–)

Dundrod 200 (1951)

Dungannon 100 (1924–27)

Enniskillen 100 (1929–52)

Greengraves (1922)

Killinchy 150 (1956–91)

Killough, Co. Down (1921)

Kirkistown (1953–)

Lisburn 100 (1946)

Long Kesh Airfield (1945)

Lurgan Park (1950–1960s)

Maghaberry (1962–74)

Mid-Antrim 100 (1940s)

Mid-Antrim 150 (1950s)

Monaghan – Glaslough circuit (1996–)

Newtownards Airport (1949–52)

North Down 60 (1925)

North West 200 (1929–)

Nutts Corner (1984–2005)

St Angelo (1960s, 2005)
Tandragee 100 (1958–)
Temple 100 (1921–99) Note: 50 first, then 60 before 100 in early 1930s
Ulster Grand Prix (1922–)
Ulster 100 (1945)

Note:

Whereas the Ulster short circuit venues are by the circuit name, the road races (eg. Temple 100, Dundrod 200) are by the event names; the latter because, in some cases, more than one course has been used.

AGHADOWEY

Aghadowey welcomed race fans and riders for its very first meeting at the County Londonderry circuit on 19 April 1975. It was described by one correspondent as the 'Armoy Armada' of Joey Dunlop, Mervyn Robinson and Frank Kennedy making the headlines as the new circuit had its baptism. It was Robinson who was really the star that day, winning not only the 350cc race, but also the main event the Embassy Championship (in both cases riding his 347cc TZ Yamaha twin), beating Joey Dunlop in the process on an identical machine. At the second Aghadowey meeting in 1975, however, Joey Dunlop scored runaway victories in both the 350 and 500cc races. Besides Dunlop, other race winners that day included Steve Cull (250cc). A third meeting at the venue completed Aghadowey's first season.

This set a pattern of three meetings per year for the following season. In 1977 this rose to four. By now Dunlop was to be found in the 250, 350, 500 and 750cc classes, with equal success and clearly a man to watch for the future.

In June 1979 Joey Dunlop set an impressive record at Aghadowey when he not only won the 'Ace of Aghadowey' title for the third year running, but also set an impressive record of five wins in five starts at the same meeting.

Irish short circuit racing in the eighties dawned with a closed-to-club meeting at Aghadowey on 5 April 1980. This was notable because it saw a victory for Joey's younger brother Robert in the 50cc event riding a Kreidler.

The promotion of the John Player Race of the Year at Aghadowey on 26 June 1982 was the most ambitious venture to date at the circuit, and some 6,000 fans turned out to see a battle royal between Honda works star Joey Dunlop and his

Programme from 1983.

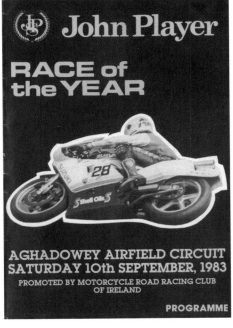

Heron Suzuki counterpart Mick Grant. There was also a strong supporting cast, including Norman Brown fresh from his Senior TT triumph. Dunlop was to win the Formula One race with ease after Grant crashed out.

A major attraction at the final meeting of 1983 was the appearance of the newly crowned British 250cc champion Neil Robinson.

Then, in September 1984 the Formula One World Champion Joey Dunlop won the John Player Race of the Year title for the third year running. Other top riders at Aghadowey during the remainder of the decade included Woolsey Coulter, Mark Farmer and Alan Irwin.

And so Aghadowey progressed. Not only had the MCRRC found a more than suitable venue to replace the defunct Maghaberry circuit but one which, in time, was not only to have a much longer time span, but would also play host to the very biggest stars in Irish racing.

ALDERGROVE AIRFIELD
The broad runways of Aldergrove Airfield were the scene of an Ulster MCC race meeting in July 1946, where Artie Bell (later a Norton works rider) took his own Norton to a double victory, winning the 500cc scratch and general handicap events.

BALLYDRAIN
Ballydrain was a typical Ulster road circuit and one of the very first, but it ran for only one year – 1922.

BALLYKELLY AIRFIELD
The former RAF station of Ballykelly made its debut as a racing circuit on the 19 July 2008, hosting the Irish Superbike Championship.

BALLYNAHINCH
In early September 1921 the Banbridge Club ran a five-lap race over the five-mile (8km) road circuit at Ballynahinch, some 15 miles (24.1km) north west of Downpatrick, Co. Down. This event was won by the Belfast rider, Herbert Chambers (AJS). Except for 1926, when events in the county were banned, Ballynahinch was used until the end of that decade.

BANBRIDGE – BANN 50
The Bann 50 – only staged in 1921 – took place over a 10-mile road circuit, near Loughbrickland, on Thursday 29 September and was won by local man James Finney (Norton). But more significantly the Bann 50 saw the race debut of the legendary Stanley Woods.

BANBRIDGE 100

Staged in the years 1928–30, the Banbridge 100 was organised by the local Banbridge club and was a typical Ulster road circuit handicap event – a single race over a 100-mile (161km) distance – over the public highway.

BANGOR CASTLE

Organised by the Ards Club in the grounds of Bangor Castle, County Down, this Ulster venue was the scene for several meetings between 1945 and 1950. Then used for one meeting early in 1966.

Large crowds, usually of between 12,000–15,000, attended, and the meetings attracted many of Ireland's top riders, including Bill Nicholson, Rex McCandless and Ernie Lyons. The course length was just over one mile (1.61km) and extremely tight, limiting lap speeds, the 500cc lap record being some 52mph (83.6km/h).

Bangor Castle programme and circuit map, 1947.

BISHOPCOURT

The Bishopcourt short circuit, near Downpatrick, County Down, was one of three short circuits in use in Ulster during the late 1960s and early 1970s. The first meeting at this venue, organised by the Mourne Motor Club, was in 1968 and they continued yearly thereafter. The first two events were for solos only, but in 1970 sidecars were included for the first time. As with many Irish races at the time, the 200cc class was popular with an interesting array

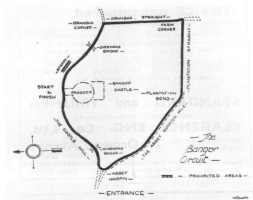

of models. In the programme of 27 June 1970 these included Bultaco, Triumph, Ducati, Suzuki, plus the odd Ariel and Villiers-engined bike. In the larger classes riders included Alex George, Cecil Crawford, Billie Guthrie and Tom Herron.

Previous winners at Bishopcourt had been Steve Murray, Tommy Robb, Brian Steenson, Bill Smith, Ken Crossett, Billie Guthrie, Campbell Gorman and Chris Goosen.

Bishopcourt programme, 1970.

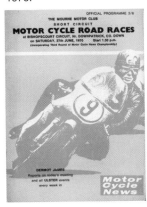

BUSH – DUNGANNON REVIVAL MEETING

First run in 2006, the 2008 Donnelly Group Bush Road Races took place on Saturday 21 June. The organisers, Dungannon & DMCC, incorporated significant resurfacing areas from the approach to Tartlagham Esses to the Cranston's Corner section of the course, with practice taking place the previous day, Friday 20 June. The Bush races, first run in 2006, are intended as a revival meeting to celebrate the long-gone Dungannon 100, which was run from 1924 until 1927.

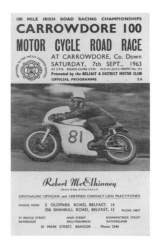

Programme, 1963.

351cc Unlimited race. Cecil Crawford leads Dennis Gallagher at Bally Boly Corner, Carrowdore 100, 1967.

Carrowdore 100

The annual Carrowdore 100 races had a history stretching back to the 1920s. They had been run on a number of different courses over the years, with the first circuit used up to the end of 1931 generally agreed to have been a difficult and potentially dangerous one.

Then, for the 1932 event, run at the end of September, the Belfast and district club ran the event over a new 13-mile (20.9km) circuit that was notable for a significant increase in speeds compared with those obtained on the old course. Riders also reported that the new course was much safer. At this time, as with many Irish events, the Carrowdore was a single handicap race. The 1932 gathering saw victory going to E. Brooks (Raleigh), a Belfast policeman.

By the 1935 event, the lap record had been raised to 75.97mph (122.23km/h), while the Excelsior factory won the team prize. Then, during the immediate post-war period the races were staged over a 10.4-mile course taking in Carrowdore, Ballywater, Dunover and back to Carrowdore.

As related under the 'Dundrod 100' section, on 23 September 1950 the Belfast club ran its 100-mile Handicap race, formally known as the 'Carrowdore', over the new Dundrod circuit. This set-up only lasted for one more season before, in September 1952, the Carrowdore name and venue returned over the previous 10.4-mile circuit.

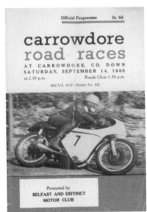

1968 circuit map and programme cover.

In 1954 the Carrowdore broke with tradition when it comprised three scratch races instead of the previous overall handicap, with 250, 350 and 500cc classes. In 1955 it was cancelled due to a late date change.

In 1956 the Carrowdore 100 returned, this time including both the scratch races and the handicap. The 500cc race winner Austin Carson (Norton) set a new lap record of 87.27mph (140.41km/h). The following year Englishman Geoff Tanner upped the record to 87.69mph (141.09km/h) and also won the Visitors Award. By September 1961 Tommy Robb (Matchless) held the record at 89.2mph (143.5km/h).

Then, in the mid-1960s the circuit length was reduced to five and a half miles (8.8km). The scratch races were all won by non-Irishmen, with Bill Smith in the 250cc (Bultaco) and Unlimited (Matchless) and the Scot Dennis Gallagher taking the 350cc on an AJS. It was the latter who set the fastest lap of the meeting at 85.56mph (137.66km/h).

CLANDEBOYE

The Clandeboye race over public roads was only staged in 1922 and as such was one of the early pioneers of such events in Ulster.

COLERAINE 100

In 1923 a single Coleraine 100 – a 100-mile (161km) handicap race – was held. Again, this was an early pioneer of this form of Ulster event, which was to remain popular until the middle part of the 20th century.

COMBER

The Belfast & District Club ran the well-known Carrowdore meeting from 1927 through to 2000. But in 1937 and 1938 the club was unable to stage it over the normal circuit so instead moved to a fresh course near Comber.

Cookstown 100, riders get
under way in the late 1950s.

Cookstown 100 programme
and map of the Sherrygrim
Circuit.

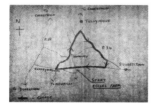

Cookstown 100

For many years the Cookstown Club of County Tyrone had the honour of
opening the Irish road-racing season. Both pre-war and immediately post-
war the famous 100-mile (161km) Handicap race was run over 13 laps of
the 7.75-mile (12.46km) rectangular Cookstown–Kildress–Oritor circuit.
The circuit ran in a clockwise direction. From the starting point,
Cookstown's mile-long, broad main street was the first side of the rectangle.
There was then a right turn to the next side, which contained two fairly
quick corners and a one-and-a-half mile (2.41km) straight to Kildress. Then
began what was known as the 'colonial section', which was exceedingly
twisty, narrow and not a good surface, particularly in the early days. After
this, a fast right corner brought competitors onto the fourth side, which
again was fast, leading back into the town and, round a wide right-hand
corner, back to the starting grid.

As this was traditionally the first race in Ulster, racing fans from all over
the north of Ireland descended on Cookstown and, as a period commentator
stated in 1950, 'On the great day there was the cheery renewing of
acquaintances to be seen everywhere.'

A feature of the Cookstown 100 Handicap was that absolutely anything
on two wheels could be used in the event. For example, the club's president
Tom Greer rode his 1926 Scott in the 1948 race. Aged 72, he led the race
for the first five laps at almost 60mph (96.5km/h) but was forced to retire
with a broken chain. Shortly after the 1949 race, he tragically lost his life in
a road accident while riding the faithful Scott. Somehow, this story portrays,
more than anything else, the true nature of the Cookstown 100.

DESERTMARTIN

The South Derry Club staged a number of motorcycle events on Wednesday 12 October 1921, including a 21-mile (33.9km) race over a 4.2-mile (6.75km) circuit at Desertmartin; this was won by J. Forsythe (Diamond – JAP).

DUNDROD 100

Since the late 1920s, the Belfast and District MCC had been using a road course at Carrowdore, County Down, for its annual 100-mile Handicap Race. In 1950, however, they gained permission to try out the then new Dundrod car circuit in County Antrim for this yearly event. This first event, run on 23 September that year, was won by W. Dempster (348cc Velocette), although the fastest lap of 75.84mph (122.02km/h) was put up by L. Carter (499cc Norton).

Although another Dundrod 100 was held in 1951, the club then switched back to its original Carrowdore venue.

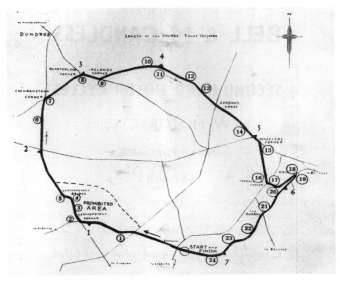

The seven-and-a-quarter-mile Dundrod road circuit.

DUNDROD 150

In 1993 the Dundrod and District MCC turned back the clock by holding the first Dundrod 150 over the famous seven-and-a-quarter-mile road circuit. In many ways this was a modern replacement for the legendary Killinchy 150, which had been run on the same circuit from 1956 through to 1991.

The meeting, held on 19 June 1993, saw a total of 11 races for machines, including 125, 200, 250, 350, 600 and 750cc. It was the two classic races that attracted the most interest, though, and riders for these included Bob Heath, Bill Swallow, Danny Shimmin, Dennis Gallagher and Colin Breeze.

Programme for the first '150' held in 1993.

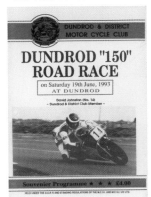

DUNDROD 200

The Dundrod 200, not to be confused with the Dundrod 100, was still organised by the same club, the Belfast and District MCC, but was a one-off affair. Held over the seven-and-a-quarter-mile (11.66km) road circuit on Saturday 30 June 1951, it was Cromie McCandless (499cc Norton) who scored not only a runaway victory in the 500cc class, but also established a new course lap record of 83.70mph (134.67km/h).

Programme for the first
Dundrod 200 from 1951.

Some 60 riders were distributed over the three scratch races, the 500cc completing 27 laps (209.25 miles – 336.68km), while the 350cc completed 25 laps and the 250cc did 23 laps. There was also a handicap award.

DUNGANNON 100

The Dungannon 100 (100-mile handicap, single race) was held over a closed-road circuit between 1924 and 1927.

ENNISKILLEN 100

The Enniskillen 100 was yet another famous long-established Ulster (County Fermanagh) long-distance handicap road race.

The three-sided Mossfield–Ballinamallard–Sydare circuit was used for this event for the first time in 1929 and, although fast, was also relatively easy to learn.

The circuit measured six and a half miles (10.5km) to a lap and ran in a clockwise direction. The nearest point of the circuit to Enniskillen was the triangle apex at Mossfield Hairpin, some three and a half miles (5.6km) north of the town. From this point, going left, there was a 0.75-mile (1.2km) straight to the starting point and pits. Around 0.15 miles (0.24km) from the start there was a slight rise, which was in effect the left into Fyffe's Corner, after which there was a short straight, followed by a right sweeping bend that ended in a sudden drop over a tiny bridge. The road then rose again for almost a mile (1.61km) to a slow right corner at Sydare.

The second side of the triangle began with a serpentine and undulating stretch of one and a half miles (2.41km) followed by a narrow, right-hand corner at Ballinamallard Village. On the last side, almost immediately there was a narrow left and then, after 0.15 miles (0.24km), a fast right corner at the Great Northern Railway Station. It was then possible to motor flat out all the way back to the very tight right through Mossfield Hairpin and then to the end of the lap.

The 1950 meeting broke with tradition, as besides the 100-mile Handicap event there was a special race for 125cc machines, which except for that year's Ulster GP was the first time this capacity class had been seen in Ireland.

1950s map of the
Enniskillen 100 course.

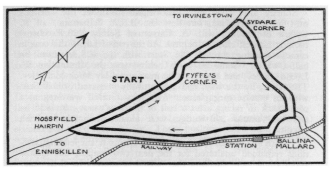

GREENGRAVES

The Greengraves (Newtownards) road race, organised by the Belfast & District Club, was only run once, in 1922. Run over a four-mile (6.5km) road course between Quarry Corner, Dundonald and the top of Bradshaws Brae, the race was held by the famous Norton rider, Jimmy Shaw, but he was destined to an early retirement on the third lap with a broken valve.

KILLINCHY 150

Many consider the annual Killinchy 150, which was run from 1956 until 1991, the finest road meeting of the Ulster national racing scene. Promoted by the Killinchy and District club, it was held over the same 7.287-mile (11.72km) Dundrod circuit as the Ulster Grand Prix (see the Ulster GP section for a description and map of the circuit).

Many riders would travel from the mainland to race at this event – mostly it has to be said for the wonderful hospitality of the Ulster people, but also to gain experience for the Grand Prix itself.

One name stood out in those early days, Liverpudlian Ralph Rensen. He won the 350cc class three years running and in his last race in 1959 won the 500cc class on his Norton. In this year he also became the first man at the Killinchy to lap at over 90mph (144.8km/h). When you consider that John Surtees on the works four-cylinder MV was only 6mph (9.6km/h) quicker with his lap record in 1959, Renson's speed was some achievement.

Other well-known riders at Killinchy in those days included Sammy Miller, Tommy Robb, Dick Creith and Bill McCosh. Later came Ralph Bryans, Brian Steenson and many more to cement the event's reputation.

KILLOUGH

Killough in County Down on 16 August 1921 was an historic date, as it marked the first motorcycle road race in Northern Ireland. With a distance of some 36 miles (58km), over three laps of a 12-mile course, it was staged as part of the local Killough sports day. As my friend Richard Agnew says in his excellent booklet *At The Centre for 100 Years* (published in 2003 to mark a century of Ulster motorcycle sport), 'Four riders started and James Stewart, riding a 4hp Harley-Davidson, won.'

KIRKISTOWN

During the late 1950s the Ulster clubs staged seven pure road races each season, but only one event was at an airfield, the September meeting organised by the Ards MCC. This was at Kirkistown and saw many of Ireland's top riders taking part.

Kirkistown programme from 15 July 1967.

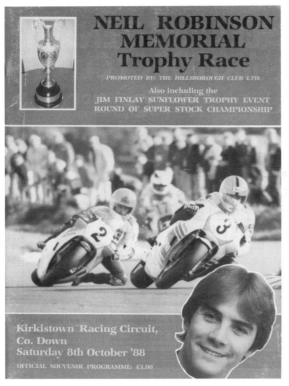

Kirkistown programme from
8 October 1988.

Kirkistown, situated near the fishing village of Portavogie on the picturesque Ards Peninsula in County Down, has been the home of the 500 Motor Racing Club of Ireland since 1953. The club, formed in 1948 to promote affordable motor racing, took its name and inspiration from the newly introduced 500cc Formula Three for small, single-seat racing cars powered by motorcycle engines.

Initially, the club had held events at Newtownards Airfield (see separate listing), but regular meetings (of both cars and bikes) caused problems for an active airfield, resulting in the club looking for a permanent base. They found an ideal home in the disused wartime airfield at Kirkistown and set about laying out a circuit. Measuring one and a half miles (2.41km), this has remained essentially the same over half a century later.

From the start a straight takes competitors to the strangely-named Debtor Dip, although no one seems to know the origins of this title. Next comes another straight leading to the right-left Colonial complex. Another straight takes riders to the long right-hander of Fisherman's (named because local fishermen in Portavogie used to hang their nets out to dry on the perimeter fence!). Then it is on to the Back Straight, originally more than 0.75-miles (1.2km) in length, and finally into the right-hand Maguire's Hairpin and back to the start–finish line.

Towards the end of the 1970s a chicane was added just before the halfway point of the Back Straight, and this has been further modified more recently.

Obviously, cars have been the priority, but motorcycles have played their part in Kirkistown history and continue to do so today. For example, in 2007 there were several bike meetings, three of which were run by the Belfast and District MCC, with the two-wheel season getting under way with a Dundrod MCC event on 17 March.

Supermoto is a recent development, and two such events were scheduled for 2007. In addition motorcycle track days are a popular feature during the summer months.

In 2004 the club began the construction of a purpose-designed clubhouse, a restaurant and bar, the latter giving panoramic views of the complete circuit.

LISBURN 100

In 1946 the Lisburn 100 handicap event took place, organised by the Lisburn & District MCC.

LONG KESH AIRFIELD

Saturday 24 November 1945 saw races held at Royal Air Force station Long Kesh, and it was believed that this was the first time an airfield had been used for motorcycle races. As with similar events that followed in mainland Britain over the immediate post-war era, the proceeds were in aid of RAF charities. Two races only were held over the three-mile (4.8km) course, each of 30 miles' (48km) distance; Bill Nicholson (BSA) won the 350cc and Artie Bell (Norton) the 500cc.

LURGAN PARK

During the late 1950s the North Armagh MCC had the distinction of being the only Irish club to promote two road races in a season. In April 1959 it promoted the second running of the Tandragee 100, and then on Saturday 1 August that year it ran a meeting over the one-mile (1.61km) circuit in Lurgan Park.

The little Lurgan track always provided interesting racing. Speeds were never high, and it was probably because of this that even 50cc machines were catered for. Again, a feature was the handicap system, which provided less well-known riders with a chance of success.

MAGHABERRY

Spring 1962 saw the first race meeting staged by the recently formed Motor Cycle Road Racing Club of Ireland and it coincided with the first-ever short circuit race at the disused airfield at Maghaberry, near Moira – then owned by Bryan Boyce – some 11 miles (17.6km) south west from Belfast. The airfield had never been used for motorcycle racing and the runways were overgrown with grass and weeds, but with the enthusiastic help of club members this was soon cleared and a reasonably sound track was made available. Such was the success of the inaugural meeting, with 96 riders participating and an attendance of approximately 2,000 spectators, that all riders had their entry monies returned. This was truly 'racing for sport'.

As for the circuit itself, this measured some one and a half miles (2.4km) in length, and at that first 1962 meeting several well-known riders featured in the day's results, including Ray McCulloch, Dick Creith and Ray Spence.

Maghaberry programme, 9 May 1964.

The second meeting at Maghaberry came at the very end of the 1963 season and saw future world champion Ralph Bryans among the entry, winning the 500cc race on a Norton. As before, there were classes for 50, 200, 250, 350 and 500cc solos, plus sidecars.

Another meeting was staged in 1964, when Patsy McGarrity led the very wet 250cc race from start to finish on an Aermacchi.

Then, after almost three years in the wilderness, racing returned to Maghaberry in 1967, when Belfast garage owner Michael McGarrity celebrated the rebirth of the circuit in great style with a hat-trick of victories.

The year 1968 saw two meetings at Maghaberry. Then in the first of three meetings at the circuit in 1969 a young Tom Herron scored his first victory there, riding a 490cc unit Triumph twin in the club Members Race. The second meeting saw Brian Steenson not only make his debut, but score a brace of wins with victories in the 350 and 500cc races and also setting the fastest lap of the day with a speed of 72.34mph (116.39km/h).

As the Motor Cycle Road Racing Club of Ireland confidently entered the 1970s, four meetings were staged at the Maghaberry circuit. It was Cecil Crawford (350 Aermacchi and 500 Norton) who was the star man. Another four meetings were staged in 1971.

Undeterred after writing off his car, Tom Herron became the first official 'Master of Maghaberry' in the first meeting of 1972. Next came a sponsorship breakthrough with WD & WO Wills Ltd, with Abe Alexander becoming the first rider to win a round of the Embassy Championship in spring 1973. A near record crowd had lined the circuit to see many of Ireland's top stars, including Ray McCullough, Ian McGregor and Billy McCosh.

The circuit changed in shape for the 1974 season. During the winter months the landowners had erected chicken sheds on the back section of the track, and thus the by now familiar figure-of-eight format had been superceded by an L-shaped track.

The second Maghaberry meeting of 1974 produced the first win at the circuit for future champion Joey Dunlop when he won the 350cc event. The swansong at Maghaberry came at the end of the 1974 season. This was because the land comprising the circuit had been earmarked for development as a prison.

MID-ANTRIM 100

The Mid-Antrim 100 was inaugurated on Wednesday 24 July 1946. Prior to that, the club had confined itself to reliability trials, including the Shame and Slemish events.

The race, said the organisers, was 'introduced purely as a sporting venture.' In spite of considerable scepticism, freely expressed, as to the wisdom of such a young club undertaking to organise a '100' motorcycle race, the race committee steadily forged ahead with its plans which proved a success right from the start.

The 1946 race was staged over a six-mile (9.65km) course at Ballygarvey, Ballymena; the distance being 100 miles (161km) and in the form of an Open Handicap. This was won by G. Dummingan (248cc Rudge), but the fastest lap of the race was achieved by the English rider Ronnie Mead (348cc Velocette).

In 1947 the Mid-Antrim 100 was held over a new and improved 10.4-mile (16.7km) circuit – still at Ballygarvey. As before, the race was a handicap, and in his second-ever road race A. McNeilly scored a runaway victory. The scratch man, Cromie McCandless (brother of Rex), managed to move up to third at the finish, establishing a record for the new course in seven minutes 29 seconds, a speed of 83.20mph (133.86km/h).

The course was, therefore, defined for future years. The first corner, McGregor's, was a slow hairpin and had to be treated with respect even by experts. Thereafter was a steep slope to the top of a ridge on the back of the course, followed by an undulating downward stretch, the surface of which, at least in the late 1940s, was considered as near perfect as possible. Just above Knockboy House was a particularly deceptive bend, and riders taking the steep downhill here at speed were forced into hard use of the brakes to negotiate Knocken Corner.

The Ballygarvey leg, from which the circuit took its name, consisted of several short straights and fast bends which led through Moat Town to the corner at Ballymena-Cushendall Road. By now riders had reached the fastest section of the course. Here there were several high-speed curves and a magnificent 'full bore' straight back to the finishing line.

MID-ANTRIM 150

Not to be confused with the earlier Mid-Antrim 100 that was held over the longer Ballygarvey circuit, the Mid-Antrim 150 was run on the six-mile (9.65km) Rathkenny course in a clockwise direction.

In an era of cigarette advertising, the Mid-Antrim 150 meeting that took place on Saturday 5 August 1975 (organised by the Mid-Antrim Motor Club) was sponsored by the Gallaher company. There were separate races for 200, 250, 350, 500 and 750cc machines. The latter machines ran concurrently with the 500s.

As for the circuit itself, the start–finish line was just before McGregor's Cross, next came the sharp hairpin-like Adam's followed by the left-right of

Mid-Antrim 100 programme and circuit plan, 1948.

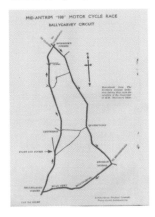

Mid-Antrim 150 programme, 1975.

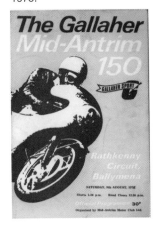

Circuit map of the Rathkenny course, used for the Mid-Antrim 150, 1975.

Newtownards programme from 1950.

1937 North West 200 programme.

Braeside. Then came another sharp right, just after Cloughwater Church. This was followed by a fast section of some two miles (3.2km) including Killyree. At the end of this came Dynbought Hairpin – the tightest corner on the circuit. After this came a series of 'S' bends, before yet another sharp right-hander. Exiting this, riders were able to accelerate on full bore to the start–finish line to complete their lap.

MONAGHAN – GLASLOUGH CIRCUIT

A recent arrival for the Ulster racing scene has been the North Monaghan Club's road circuit at Glaslough. The first such meeting was staged on 25 August 1996, with Derek Young scoring a hat-trick of victories.

NEWTOWNARDS AIRPORT

The Knock Motor Cycle Club put on short circuit races at Newtownards Airport during the early post-World War Two period with the cooperation of the North of Ireland Aero Club. There were both scratch and handicap events. The first such event was staged in 1949.

The meeting there on Saturday 22 July 1950 came after official practice the previous evening saw both W.A.C. McCandless (Norton) and R.T. Matthews (Velocette) both equal Artie Bell's lap record. By the end of the meeting McCandless had created a new one. The circuit length was 1.38 miles (2.22km).

NORTH DOWN 60

The North Down 60 (60-mile handicap) was only run once, in 1925. Why? Well, at one of the club's earlier events (a speed trial at Clandeboye in 1923) a spectator had been killed. And this was to see a court action, the result being a ban on racing in 1926 by the Down County Council. Although this ban was subsequently lifted in spring 1927, the North Down Club had by then been forced to close.

NORTH WEST 200

With the exception of the Ulster Grand Prix, the North West 200 was by far the biggest road race in Ulster.

The race began in 1929 and continues to the present day, being run over the well-known triangular, anti-clockwise Portstewart–Coleraine–Portrush circuit, which for many years measured 11.1 miles (17.9km) to the lap.

The very first winner of the opening North West 200 handicap race way back in 1929 was Willie-John McCracken on a 348cc Velocette, and his fastest lap was at over 67mph (117.8km/h). He was later to become a

Harold Daniel (Norton), just beats Freddie Frith (Velocette) in the 1949 350cc race North West 200, one of the closest finishes ever in the event.

Programme from 1949, and a map of the course.

successful Belfast businessman, with spells as high sheriff of Belfast and deputy lord mayor of the city.

Originally the pits and starting grid were placed on a wide road opposite the York Hotel on Portstewart, and from there competitors almost immediately negotiated the narrow 90-degree left Harry's Corner onto the town's long promenade. Rising from there were two slowish, walled corners followed by a narrow but fast section, which dropped suddenly to the wide plantation S-bend. Two more fairly fast corners at the fourth milestone led to Millburn Hairpin on the outskirts of Coleraine. The second side of the triangle began at this point and led up to the deceptive right-left S-bend of Shell Hill Bridge, after which there were approximately four miles of full bore over the hill and down towards Metropole Corner in Portrush. The final side of the triangle, from this sharp left corner back to the starting point, ran along the rugged northern coast of Ulster and was twisty and undulating, testing rider ability, braking and acceleration in equal measure.

It should be noted that over the years the course was altered and improved in detail. This meant that comparing lap speeds is somewhat pointless. Additionally, up to 1959 there was one single 200-mile (322km) race, but from 1960 onwards there were separate races. For example, that first year there were

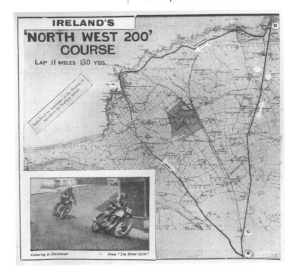

Alan Shepherd was a double winner of the North West 200 during 1962, winning the 350 and 500cc races on AJS and Matchless machines respectively. He is seen here entering the Portstewart Promenade on his larger bike.

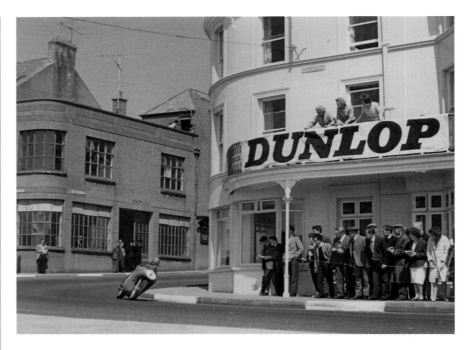

Programme from 1959.

Programme from 1962.

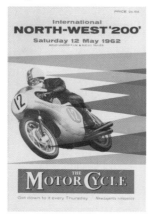

three events, for the 250, 350 and 500cc. The distance for each class varied with five laps for 250, seven for 350, and nine for 500cc.

The next milestone came in 1964, when the Coleraine and District Motor Club replaced the previous event organisers, the North of Ireland Motor Club (the latter having said that the North West was no longer financially viable). The Coleraine Club proved them wrong, and the races went back to their former glory. In 1973 the circuit length was changed to 10.1 miles (16.2km) and that same year the 250, 350 and 500cc classes were joined by a new 750cc category.

Next, in 1977, Englishman Tony Rutter became the first man in the North West's history to have won all four capacity classes when he won the 500cc race on Harold Coppick's Suzuki RG four-cylinder two-stroke. Previously, Tony had won the 250 in 1973 and 1977, the 350 in 1973, 1978 and 1979, and the 750 in 1978.

In fact, the list of winners in the North West is akin to a who's who of motorcycle racing and includes the likes of Eric Fernihough, Jimmy Guthrie, Stanley Woods, Harold Daniell, Geoff Duke, Bob McIntyre, Sammy Miller, Alan Shepherd, Derek Minter, Ralph Bryans, Peter Williams, Rod Gould, John Cooper, Paul Smart, Mick Grant and Joey Dunlop.

Now, at the beginning of the 21st century, Superbikes is the most important category, but other classes also attract excellent grids.

During many years of the North West's history, crowds numbering in excess of 100,000 have often turned out to see this historic event. In days gone by the North West 200 was graced by the world's best riders. But today, as with the Ulster GP and Isle of Man TT, this is no longer the case. It still remains a popular event and is well-supported by riders both from Ireland itself and the rest of the British Isles.

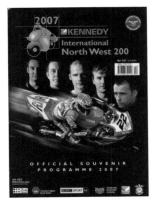

Programme from 2007.

NUTTS CORNER
Nutts Corner held a number of race meetings between 1984 and 2005.

ST ANGELO
The St Angelo airfield, Enniskillen, was one of the few short circuits in use in Ulster during the 1960s, but today it is almost forgotten by all except the keenest enthusiasts for the sport of motorcycle racing.

TANDRAGEE 100
Measuring five and a half miles (8.8km) in length, the Tandragee 100 meeting was first staged in April 1958 and was organised by the North Armagh club. The road course ran between Tandragee and Markethill, County Armagh. Situated some 30 miles (48.3km) south west of Belfast, the event attracted the likes of Neol Orr, Len Ireland and Ralph Rensen for that first 1958 event. In traditional Irish style at that time, the main race was a handicap with subsidiary class awards. After 18-laps (99 miles – 159.3km) Neol Orr (Matchless) won from George Purvis (BSA) and Len Ireland (348cc Norton).

For the 1959 event it is interesting to recall that a certain Ralph Bryans (197cc Ambassador) won the 200cc category.

Tandragee 100 programme and circuit plan from 1963.

TEMPLE 100
The Temple club's annual 100-mile (161km) road race was run over a variety of different circuits since the very first on Saturday 3 September 1921. Then, it was a much shorter affair, with riders and machines covering 11-laps of a 2.25-miles circuit, which in terms of distance amounted to some 25 miles (36.2km). The start was at Temple Crossroads, followed by a left turn at the Church Corner, a difficult ride along a twisty section towards Prentice's Corner, a further left turn and then back to the Temple to begin the next lap.

By the early 1930s a longer pear-shaped 5.7-mile (9.2km) circuit, which was generally agreed to be one of the most difficult of all Ulster road courses, was developed. Starting at Broadmills, almost halfway along one side of the 'pear', the course ran over a fast main road for a distance of some 1.6 miles (2.6km) to the wide, but nonetheless slowish, right-hand corner at

Programme from 1976.

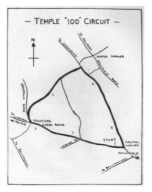

The 1968 Saintfield circuit.

Len Ireland (350cc Aermacchi-Metisse) negotiating a tight hairpin bend, Temple 100, late 1960s.

Drummalig. It then turned on to a narrow back road with a very short straight and then a sharp right-hand bend near the second milestone. From this point back to Prentice's Crossroads, another couple of miles distance, it was rather bumpy, and there were several narrow twists and turns where lower gears were in constant use. At the crossroads there were some particularly bad bumps that could put riders off the right line for the next bend. After that the road improved, going on past the school to the first side once again at the fairly fast right-hand Church Corner. The remaining half-mile or so back to the start line was particularly fast.

The first 100-miler was staged in 1933 and the last in 1966. Traditionally, the Temple 100 was held at the end of July, and by the late 1960s the races were being held over the five-and-a-half-mile (8.8km) Saintfield circuit, which used some of the old circuit but was now triangular, rather than pear-shaped. Also by then the meeting had introduced separate shorter scratch races, rather than the original single 100-mile handicap event.

In 1966 there were classes for 50cc (four laps), 200cc (five laps), 250cc (nine laps), 350cc (nine laps) and 500cc (nine laps). Hero of the day was Ray McCullough, who sliced five seconds off Tommy Robb's 250cc lap record in beating Englishman Trevor Burgess and his very fast Woolley-tuned Greeves Silverstone. Riding a Bultaco, McCullough's new record stood at 81.15mph (130.05km/h), compared to Tommy's 1959 lap of 79.52mph (127.94km/h).

ULSTER GRAND PRIX

Notable motorcycle enthusiast and Ulster Member of Parliament the late Thomas Moles assisted in pushing through parliament the first Road Races Act which made it legal for the Clady course to be closed to the public for the inaugural Ulster Grand Prix staged on 14 October 1922. That initial race had a total of 75 entries in four classes (250, 350, 600cc solos and sidecars).

1937 programme and map showing the original long Clady Circuit.

In 1926 the 500cc race was won by Graham Walker (father of Murray) on a Sunbeam. He also went on to win the 1928 Senior event on a Rudge.

For 1936 the *Federation Internationale Motorcycliste* gave Ulster the title of Grand Prix of Europe, an honour which was to be repeated in 1948. When the World Championships arrived for the 1949 season, the Ulster Grand Prix was included among the calendar, a position the event held right up to 1971. But, sadly, the worsening political situation in Northern Ireland forced the promoters to cancel the 1972 event, and with the lobby against the dangers of pure road racing gaining momentum all the time Championship status was destined never to return.

Nevertheless, together with the Isle of Man Tourist Trophy and the North West 200, the Ulster Grand Prix is still considered to be one of the three greatest true 'road' races still in existence.

From 1922 until 1939 the event was staged over the legendary 20.5-mile (32.98km) long Clady Circuit, including the notoriously bumpy seven-mile (11.26km) straight. At this time it ran across part of the grass runway at the Royal Air Force Station, Aldergrove.

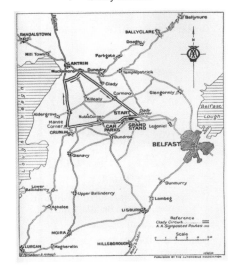

Competitors getting underway at the start of the 1930 Ulster GP in which water caused the retirement of several riders.

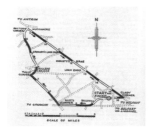

The shorter post-war Clady circuit.

Alterations to this part of the circuit during World War Two resulted in a new, shorter post-war Clady circuit measuring 16.5 miles (26.5km) to a lap, used from 1947 until 1952. In 1953 the event was transferred to the nearby Dundrod road course, this being some 7.401 miles (11.908km) in length. Because of the length of the three circuits involved it is suggested that the reader consults the relevant maps printed in this book, so that each circuit can be analysed.

During the 1920s, besides Graham Walker, the Ulster GPs top star riders included Wal Handley, Alex Bennett, Charlie Dodson and Joe Craig, the

Austrialian Eric McPherson AJS 7R (37) leads his countryman Harry Hinton (Manx Norton) at Nutts Corner, during the 1950 Ulster GP. Staged over the Clady Circuit (famous for its seven-mile straight), McPherson eventually came home in fourth place in the 13-lap, 214.5-mile race.

The 1955 Ulster GP, Dundrod, 350cc race. John Surtees, Norton (2); Cecil Sandford, Moto Guzzi (23).

latter to win greater fame as the Norton factory's race supremo from the late 1920s until his retirement in the mid-1950s.

Into the 1930s a new set of names were to appear in the Ulster's entry lists, with Stanley Woods, Jimmy Guthrie, Jimmy Simpson, Walter Rusk, Jock West and Dorino Serafini being among the winners.

The late 1940s and 1950s witnessed greats such as Freddie Frith, Les Graham, Artie Bell, Geoff Duke, Ken Kavanagh, Ray Amm, Bill Lomas, Carlo Ubbiali and John Surtees. As the 1950s turned into the 1960s yet more names arrived on the scene, notably Bob McIntyre, Alastair King, Gary Hocking and Mike Hailwood. By the mid-1960s these had been joined by Jim Redman, Phil Read, Bill Ivy and Giacomo Agostini.

During its history the Ulster has seen much controversy. In the 1936 Lightweight (250cc) event, Ginger Wood and Bob Foster, both riding New Imperial machines, crossed the finishing line so close together that even after over 200 miles (321.8km) of racing it took the judges an hour to decide that Wood was the winner by a mere one-fifth of a second! Then in 1939, due to

The 1970 Ulster GP,
Dundrod, Rod Gould (2)
leads Kent Andersson (3),
both on Yamahas.

Plan of the Dundrod circuit.

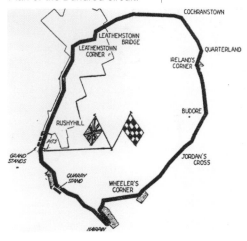

the international situation, the Grand Prix was almost called off, but in spite of an entry of only 60 riders, it did take place. And what a meeting it was too. Not only did Irishman Walter Rusk set the first over 100mph (161km/h) lap in Grand Prix history (riding a supercharged AJS V-four), but the Italian Gilera rider Dorino Serafini won the 500cc race. It was the last Grand Prix to be staged in Europe before the outbreak of war a few weeks later.

In more modern times the Ulster Grand Prix has produced some superb races, and even after it had lost its World Championship status still attracted the likes of Tom Herron, Ron Haslam, John Williams and the South African Jon Ekerold in the 1970s, while the 1980s saw the emergence of stars like Mick Grant, Brian Read, Wayne Gardner, Steve Hislop and Carl Fogarty. But it has been Joey Dunlop (24 victories) and Phillip McCallan (14 victories) whose names head the winners listings (up to the end of 2007).

A special mention should be made to Joey Dunlop who for many years was 'King of the Roads'. His record 24 wins at the Ulster spanned three decades – his first in 1979 and his last in 1999.

In 2007 the Grand Prix attracted 162 riders, including no less than 38 new to the course, and the event which took place on 18 August was sponsored by *The Belfast Telegraph* newspaper.

Finally, except for the World War Two years, the event has always been run, apart from in 1972 when it was cancelled because of the political situation in Northern Ireland, and in 2001 during the foot-and-mouth crisis.

ULSTER 100

On Saturday 22 September 1945 the Ulster Motor Cycle Club ran the first post-war road race – the Ulster 100 – over a five-mile (8km) circuit, utilising parts of the Lisburn–Dundrod and Lisburn–Glenavy roads. As with many other Ulster road events at the time, this was a handicap event, the winner being Harry Jackson.

Ulster GP programme from 1970.

APPENDIX

Circuit/Events in Southern Ireland (Eire)

Ardcloyne, used for Munster 100, 1977–81, 1985.

Athboy (1965–66)

Athea (2002–)

Athy 75 (1925–30)

Ballybunion (2005), racing cancelled after fatal accident.

Carrigrohane, first event on 3.5-mile circuit in 1947, 6-mile circuit used for Munster 100 from 1950–55.

Clane, Co. Kildare (1932–33)

Clonakilty, used for Munster 100, 1989–92.

Curragh, short circuit 1947–67; long circuit 1947 only.

Dunboyne, venue for Leinster 200 from 1958–67.

Dundalk:

    Riverstown circuit (1990)

    Louth Village (1991–96)

    Togher (1997)

    Dundalk By-pass 1 (1998–99)

    Darver (2000–06)

    Dundalk By-pass (2007)

Dunshaughlin, Leinster 100, first circuit 1923, second circuit used from 1924–26 and in 1929.

Elphin, (1991), the race did not run as officials decided the road surface was not suitable.

Faugheen (1976–86)

Fore, first event 1973; race transferred to Walderstown in 2000.

Kells (Dunlane, Crossakiel)

Killalane, first event 1984.

Leitrim Village (1984–86, 1997–98)

Leinster 200, various venues and dates – see other entries.

Monahan Circuit (Cork City) (1940–55)

Mondello Park, first motorcycle meeting Leinster 200, 25 May 1968.

Munster 100, various venues and dates – see other entries.

Phoenix Park, first event 1924. Dublin 100, 1931–40. Oldtown circuit; Hawthorn circuit; Leinster 100 1927–28.

Rathdrum (1962–73)

Rathgormack (1970–72)

Skerries, used from 1930–35 for Leinster 200; from 1946 onwards used for annual Skerries 100.

Straffon, Co. Kildare (1931–32)

Tallaght, venue for Leinster 200 1936 onwards revived after the war 1948–49.

Tullyallen (1965–66), revived in 2006 as Boyne 100 using only part of the original circuit.

Walderstown (2000–)

Wicklow, venue for Leinster 200 from 1950–57.

INDEX

Aberaman Motor Club 137–39
Aberdare Park 137–39, 144
Aberdeen 121, 12–26, 130
ACC 11–12
Acme, Rex 151, 156
ACU (Auto-Cycle Union) 17–18,
    33, 39, 41, 43, 53–54, 58, 63,
    79, 83, 95, 97, 100, 103, 108,
    115, 117, 136
Aermacchi 78, 82, 96–97, 117–18,
    126, 144, 178
AFN 42–43
Aghadowey 166–68
Agnew, Richard 10, 175
Agostini, Giacomo 22, 73, 75, 83,
    91–92, 105, 158, 187
Agricultural Disaster Fund 36
Aintree Club Circuit 109
Aintree Motorcycle Racing Club
    10
AJS 17–18, 30, 36, 39, 40, 50,
    52–53, 70, 76, 78, 81, 87, 96,
    113–14, 118, 122, 125, 141–42,
    145, 152, 154, 156, 168, 171,
    182, 186, 188
Aladana, Dave 116
Aldergrove Airfield 166, 168
Alexander, Abe 178
Alexandra Palace 9, 14–15
Alford 121
Allan, Robbie 127, 130
Altcar 108, 110–11
Alton Towers 9, 58–60
Ambrosini, Dario 158
American Indy Car racing 79
Anderson, Bob 40, 82, 152
Anderson, Fergus 18, 40, 61
Andersson, Kent 83, 188
Andreas 150, 154
Andreas Racing Association 150
Andrews, Nick 94
Anglesey 137, 140, 145, 149
Angus 129, 133

Ansty 58, 60–62
Antelope MCC 60–61
Appleyard, Colin 97
Archer, Les Jnr 47, 52, 56, 141
Ardcloyne 190
Ards Club 169
Ards MCC 175
Ards Peninsula 176
Armstrong, Reg 108
Arnold, Dave 36
Arter, Tom 14
Ashbourne 58, 62
Ashton, Dean 105
Ashton-in-Makerfield 119
ASPS 71
Athea 190
Australia 26
Auto Cycle Club 11
Aylesbury 69–70
Baaregarroo 160
Bailey, David 33
Baldwin, O.M. 24
Ballacarrooin 165
Ballacraine 156, 160
Ballado 121
Ballakeighan 153
Ballaorris 153
Ballaugh 151, 160
Ballaugh Cronk 151
Ballavarran Road 151
Ballinamallard Village 174
Ballington, Kork 83
Ballwhetstone 153
Bally Boly Corner 170
Ballybunion 190
Ballydrain 166, 168
Ballygarvey 179
Ballykelly Airfield 166, 168
Ballymena 179
Ballynahinch 166, 168
Ballywater 170
Banbridge Club 168–69
Bangor Castle 9, 166, 169

Barawanath 25
Barkston Heath 85
Barn Corner 90
Barnett, Sid 16, 31, 39, 42, 53,
    61–62, 69, 87, 104, 110, 138,
    141–42
Barnsley 111
Barry Motor Club 144, 147
Barry, Geoff 34
Bateman, Steve 36, 55
Bates, Vic 10
Bath 45
Battle of Britain 15, 29
Bayley, J.W. 147
Bayliss, Len 62, 68
BBC 54, 93, 104, 122, 139
Beadnell 85–86
Beasley, Doug 31, 90
Bedford, Steve 10
Beeton, Jackie 61, 86, 89
Belfast 168, 170–71, 173, 175–78,
    181, 183, 189
Belfast & District Club 171, 175
Belgium 61
Bell, Artie 157, 168, 177, 180, 187
Belle Vue 108, 111
Bellers-Smith, Jay 148
Bemsee 70
Benelli 82, 160
Bennett, Alex 186
Bennett, Dave 52–54, 138
Bermondsey 18
Bettison, Peter 107
Beveridge Park 121–23
Beveridge, Michael 122
Beverley 95
Bicknell, C.B. 25
Biggin Hill 14–15
Billown 153, 155, 165
Bills, Ken 152
Birks, Chas 43
Birmingham 157
Bishop's Waltham 53
Bishopcourt 166, 169
Bisset, Tom 31–32
Blackburn 86, 88, 112
Blackburn Welfare Motor Club 86

Blackmore Vale Club 38, 40–41
Blair, J. 125
Blandford 38–40
Blandford Camp 38–40

BMW 40, 157
Boddice, Bill 16, 18, 20, 29, 34,
    41–42, 46, 62, 68, 88, 148
Boddice, Mick 43, 63
Bollington, J. 113
Bolton 112
Border Motor Racing Club 86, 102,
    124
Boreham 14–18
Boreham Aerodrome 16
Bourton-on-the-Water 48
Bowes-Lyon, Lady Elizabeth 71
Boyce, Bryan 177
Bradden Bridge 160
Brader, Brian 37
Bradford 99–100
Bradshaws Brae 175
Brands Hatch 9, 14, 18–22, 33,
    35, 47, 66–67, 73, 78, 93, 115
Brandywell 161
Bray Hill 114, 156, 165
Brechin 129
Brecon 140
Breeze, Colin 173
Brett, Jack 86–87, 101, 108
Bridlington 93, 95
Briggs, Alf 60, 76
Briggs, Eric 31
Briggs, Molly 76
Bristol 41, 45, 72
Bristol MCC 45
Bristol Motor Cycle and Light Car
    Club 41
British Automobile Racing Club
    (BARC) 73, 146
British car GP 83
British Championship 54–55, 93,
    115, 133
British Championships 54, 115
British Motor Cycle Racing Club
    (BMCRC) 25, 29, 32, 69–70,
    80, 82–83, 113

British Motorcycle Grand Prix 66, 83

British Racing Drivers' Club (BRDC) 81

British Superbike Championship 22, 35, 56, 75, 79, 93, 98, 116, 135, 146

British Touring Car Championships 135

Broadmills 183

Brooklands 9, 13–14, 22–26, 32, 37, 63, 80, 146

Brooklands Automobile Racing Club 13

Brooks, E. 170

Brough 26, 85–88

Brough Airfield 87

Brown, Bob 61, 159

Brown, George 16, 29, 31, 36, 61–62, 69–70, 87, 90, 104, 107, 141

Brown, Jimmy 80

Brown, Norman 168

Browning, Dave 51

Browning, Don 51

Brownlee, Adam 127

Bruce, Charlie 123–24, 126, 130

Bryans, Ralph 175, 178, 182–83

Bryanston Park 9, 38, 40–41

BSA 19, 34–35, 52–53, 76, 78, 107, 121, 131–32, 136, 147, 177, 183

BTCC Touring Cars 98

Buchan, George 97, 117–18, 126

Buchan, Jimmy 123, 126, 131, 152

Buith Wells 140

Bullock, Jack 102

Bultaco 97, 169, 171, 185

Burgen, Les 48

Burgess, Trevor 78, 97, 185

Burry Port 146

Burton, C.F. 'Squib' 63

Butcher, Derek 135

Cadger, Agnes 10

Cadwell Park 9, 22, 67, 85, 89–92, 101, 116

Camathias, Florian 105

Cammock, Brian 'Snowy' 112

Campbell circuit 25

Campbell, K. 143

Cann, Maurice 28–29, 34, 36, 39, 42, 46–47, 53, 56, 69, 72, 81, 84, 90, 100, 103, 113, 141, 152

Cannell, Graham 111

Canning Town 9, 12

Canterbury 31

Cardiff 147

Carlisle 117

Carmarthen Motor Clubs 140

Carnaby 85, 93–95

Carnaby Two 95

Carr, Louis 145

Carrigrohane 190

Carrowdore 166, 170–71, 173

Carson, Austin 171

Carter, Chris 62

Carter, Fred 65

Carter, L. 173

Carter, P.H. 42

Cartwright, Dave 36

Cass, Kevin 97

Castle Combe 10, 38, 41–44

Castle Combe Circuit Ltd 44

Castletown 153–54

Castletown Square 156

Catlin, George 59

Catterick Airfield 85, 95–96

Catterick Camp 85, 96

Caxton 30

Chambers, Herbert 168

Chapman, Brian 68

Charterhall 121, 124, 136

Cheeson, Bill 19, 31

Chelmsford 15–17

Cheltenham Motor Club 48, 50–52, 70

Chester 113

Chilton, Neil 37

Chippenham 41, 45

Chirk Castle 58, 62

Chivenor 38, 44

Christie, G.B. 132

Clady Circuit 185–86

Clandeboye 166, 171, 180

Clark, Brian 96, 102
Clark, Nigel 10
Classic Racing Motorcycle Club
    (CRMC) 32, 129, 140, 146
Clatchymore 132
Claxton, Jack 103
Clay Hill 114
Clayton, C.L. 27
Cleveland 106
Clonakilty 190
Clypse Circuit 150, 159, 164
Coleman, Rod 108
Coleraine 166, 171, 181–82
Coleraine Club 182
Colerne 38, 45
Colerne Aerodrome 45
Collier, Charlie 24, 156
Combe 10, 38, 41–44
Conn, Chris 147–48
Cook, W. 24
Cookstown 166, 172
Cookstown Club 172
Cooper, John 22, 60, 83, 92, 97,
    104–05, 116, 126, 148, 182
Cooper, Leslie 122, 130
Corby 79
Cork 190
Coronation Day race 89
Coronation Grand Prix 27
Cott, Paul 95
County Londonderry circuit 167
Coupland 84
Coventry 60–61
Cowbridge 144
Craig, Joe 186
Crail 121, 124–25, 132
Craner 64, 66
–, 170, 178
Creg-ny-Baa 161, 165
Creg-ny-Mona 163
Creith, Dick 175, 177
Creith, John 139
Crimond 121, 125–26
Croft 85, 97–98
Croft Autodrome 97
Cronk-ny-Mona 165
Cronk-y-Voddee 160

Crookbain, Jeff 36
Crookhall, A.B. 151
Crosby, Graeme 105, 162
Crosier, Bill 96–97, 129
Cross Fourways hairpin 153
Crossakiel 190
Crossett, Ken 169
Crossier, Bill 118, 131
Croxford, Dave 55, 105, 116
Cruden Bay 126
Crystal Palace 14–15, 26–27
CTS 65
Cull, Steve 167
Culzean Castle 136
Cumbrian MCRC 119
Curry, Jim 49
Dale, Dickie 29, 62, 69, 104, 108,
    142
Daniell, Harold 25–27, 32, 39, 61,
    65, 84, 152, 157, 181–82
Daniels, J.D. 141
Darley Moor 58, 62–63
Darlington 95, 97
Darver 190
Darvill, Peter 34
Davey, Peter 75–6, 90
Davies, Bob 44
Davies, T. 62
Davis, Barry 78
Davis, Dave 94
Davis, Ted 34
Degens, Dave 42
Dempster, W. 173
Denley, George 24
Denton, Ben 100
Denton, J. 59
Derby Cup 75–76
Derbyshire Royal Infirmary 64
Deubel, Max 105
Devizes 48
Diamond Jubilee TT 158
Dickie, Tom 127
Dickinson, Gary 49, 102
Difazio, Jack 41, 47
Difazio, Richard 51
Ditchburn, Barry 28
Dixon, Freddie 24

DMW 62
Dobbie, Denis 135
Dodson, Charlie 111, 186
Doncaster 76
Donington Hall 64
Donington Park 58, 63, 65, 67, 83
Doran, Bill 29, 53, 69, 87, 110
Dorchester 93
Douglas 13, 151–52, 159
Downpatrick 168, 169
Drummalig 184
Ducati 43, 71, 78, 82, 96, 102,
    113, 115, 133, 147, 159, 169
Dudley-Ward, Allan 41–42, 89–90
Duffus, Alan 125, 127
Duffus, Ian 111
Dugdale, Alan 45, 62, 78
Dugdale, Hector 62
Duke, Geoff 19, 29, 39, 46,
    53–54, 61, 69, 81, 87, 103–04,
    108, 111–12, 152, 182, 187
Dulman, Boet Van 66
Dumfries 126
Dummingan, G. 179
Dundalk By-pass 190
Dundee and Angus Motor Club
    130, 133
Dundonald 175
Dundrod 166–67, 171, 173–76,
    186–88
Dunfermline 134
Dungannon & DMCC 169
Dungannon Revival Meeting 166,
    169
Dunholme 47, 69–70, 80, 85
Dunholme Hutchinson Hundred
    Handicap 47
Dunlane 190
Dunlop, Joey 92, 105, 119, 164,
    167–68, 178, 182, 188
Dunover 170
Dunphy, Joe 28, 83
Dunshaughlin 190
Dunstall 57
Earl Shilton 72
East Fortune 121, 126–29
East Lothian 126

East Midlands Centre
    Championship 59–60
East Mountain Gate 161
East Yorkshire Borough Council
    94
Easthaven 133
Eastough, Dave 92
Eboracum Motor Club 98
Eccleshall 100
Ecclestone, Bernie 19, 83
Eckert, Johnny 59
Edinburgh 124, 127, 133
Edward VII 11
Edwards, Dave 10, 110
Edzell 121, 129–30
Eire 7, 190
Ekerold, Jon 188
Ellison, Dean 44
Elvington 85, 98–99
Elvington Park Club 99
Elvington Park National 99
EMC 47
Emmett, Sean 44
Ennett Memorial 156
Enniskillen 7, 166, 174, 183
Eppynt 137, 140–42, 148
Errol 121, 130–32
Errol Aerodrome 130
Esholt 85, 99–100
Euro Challenge Super Moto 101
Everett, Reg 10
Everthorpe Park 85, 101
Evesham 70
Fairwood 137, 143
Fairwood Aerodrome 143
Fakenham 33, 37
Falmouth Harbour 51
Farmer, Mark 168
Farrant, Derek 40, 108
Fath, Helmut 40, 105
FB Mondial 18, 115
Featherbed Nortons 61, 100
Featherstone, Mick 29, 87
Federation Internationale
    Motorcycliste 185
Ferbrache, Peter 59–60, 76
Fernihough, Eric 25, 182

Festival of Britain 54, 87, 111
Festival of Britain Championship
    87
Festival of Yesteryear 104
Fife 122–25, 134–35
Filtrate Trophy 117
FIM Sidecar World Championship
    44
Findlay, John 127, 129
Findo Gask 132
Finney, James 168
Firth of Tay 130
Fitapaldi, Emerson 35
Fitton, Rob 96–97, 104
Fleetwood 112
Fletcher, Frank 110
Flookburgh 108, 111
Fogarty, Carl 43, 83, 105, 188
Fogarty, George 95
Ford Motor Company 18
Formula Five 111
Formula One 19, 32, 43, 168
Formula Two 129, 148
Forsythe, J. 173
Foster, Bob 39, 41, 46–47, 56, 61,
    65, 103, 141, 152, 187
Foulston, Nicola 35
Foulston, John 22
Fowler, Rem 156
France 61
Freeman, Charlie 154
French, Andrew 49
Frith, Freddie 65, 100, 152, 157,
    181, 187
Froickheim 133
Fry, Frank 36
Furneaux Special 131
Furneaux, J. 131
Gallagher, Dennis 102, 123, 131,
    133, 170–71, 173
Gamston 58, 68
Gardner, Wayne 105, 188
Gask 121, 132–33
Gaydon 57–58, 68–69
Geeson, R.E. 152
George, Alex 97, 127, 169
George, John 127, 129

Gerard, Bob 72
Germany 12, 157
Gilbert, E. Harris 132
Gilera 19, 109, 188
Gittins, Ian 36
Glaslough 166, 180
Glen Auldyn 160
Glen Helen 156, 160
Glencrutchery Road 159, 163, 165
Godfrey, O.C. 24
Godfrey, Tony 36, 42
Gold Cup 67, 104–05
Gold Cup International 105
Gooch, Rodney 10, 44
Good, Robin 145
Goodfellow, David 119
Goodhall, Roy 95
Goodman, Peter 31, 41, 61
Goodwood 14, 16, 29–30
Goodwood Revival Meeting 29
Goole 101
Goosen, Chris 169
Gorman, Campbell 169
Gosling Stadium 37
Goss, Neville 53
Gould, Rod 182, 188
Gow, Jack 121, 124, 131, 133
Graham, Les 17–18, 36, 39, 54,
    69, 81, 90, 114, 141–42, 187
Graham, Rae 126
Graham, Roy 132, 161
Graham, Stuart 78, 128
Grampian Motorcycle Convention
    121
Grandsden Lodge Airfield 30
Gransden Lodge 9, 14
Grant, Mick 83, 92, 98, 105, 110,
    116, 123, 133, 162, 168, 182,
    188
Grantham 84–85
Gravesend Eagles 19
Great North Road 79, 95
Greenwood, Owen 97
Greer, Tom 172
Greeves Hall Project 108, 112
Griffiths, Selwyn 50, 117, 138–39,
    145, 148

Grindley, Howard 59, 76
Grindley-Pearless-JAP 25
Grove Hall 79
Grovewood Securities 21, 35, 66, 73
Gruber, Wolfgang 10
Guthrie Memorial 161
Guthrie, Billie 169
Guthrie, Jimmy 182, 187
Haddenham 58, 69, 70
Haddington 126
Hagon, Alf 19
Hailwood, Mike 15, 21, 28, 34, 42, 75, 82, 92, 105, 115, 138, 158–160, 187
Halford, Major F.B. 24
Hall, Ginger 160
Hallamshire Motor Club 68
Halsall, Wilf 150
Handley, Wal 24, 186
Hanley Park 58, 70
Hanley Park Horticultural Show 70
Hardy, E.V.C. 152
Harfield, Len 36
Hargreaves, Bernard 68, 123
Harley-Davidson 24, 175
Harris, Pip 18, 28, 41, 46–47, 53–54, 68, 105
Harris, Ron 25
Hartle, John 82–83, 105, 115, 152
Hartog, Will 105
Haslam, Phil 153
Haslam, Ron 110, 188
Haswell, J.R. 24
Havland, Harry 10
Hawthorn circuit 190
Heath, Bob 173
Heath, Prees 58, 78
Heckles, Keith 62, 78, 147
Hele-Shaw, Doctor 12
Hennan, Pat 92
Hepworth, M. 94
Herne Hill 9
Heron Suzuki 116, 168
Herron, Tom 169, 178, 188
Heuwen, Keith 105

Hill, Tommy 44
Hillaby, Peter 10, 106
Hillberry 163, 165
Hillhead 102
Hinton, Harry 186
Hislop, Steve 188
Hobson, Mac 97, 127
Hocking, Gary 187
Hockley, Austin 95
Hodgkin, J.P.E. 16, 52
Hodgkin, John 59, 76
Hogan, John 34, 41, 46, 52–53
Holly Wood 64–65
Honda 34, 42–43, 62, 71, 78, 82, 92, 97, 117, 123, 133, 139, 146, 149, 158, 164, 167
Horn, Colin 46, 86–87
Horncastle 89
Horseman, Jack 117
Horsforth 107
Horsham, Phil 37
Horsman, Victor 24
Horton, P.H. 148
Housley, Eric 68
Huggett, Fred 36
Hull 86, 101, 107
Hungary 25
Hunt, Tim 151
Huxley, Derek 146
Hyde Park 26
Ibsley 38, 46
Ibsley Airfield 46
Imber Road 38, 47, 52
Indy Circuit 21
Ingliston 121, 133
International Cup Race 12
International Grand Prix 65
International Road Racing Club 27
International Six Days Trial 65
Ireland Aero Club 180
Ireland, Len 183–84
Irish Superbike Championship 168
Irwin, Alan 168
Isle of Man 9, 11, 13, 22, 32, 63, 76, 112, 115, 128, 150–51, 153, 155, 157, 159, 161, 163, 183, 185

Isle of Man Tourist Trophy 12–13, 22, 32, 63–64, 105, 111, 114, 138–39, 150–153, 156–165, 168, 183, 185
Italy 12
Ivy, Bill 37, 42, 92, 138, 187
Jackson, Harry 189
JAP 60, 76, 173
Jefferies, Allan 100
Jefferies, Nick 95
Jefferies, Tony 98
Jim Russell Racing School 34
John Player International 83
Johnson, Dean 93
Johnson, Eddie 97, 117
Jolly, Steve 78
Judd, Rex 24
Junior Racing Association 120
Jurby 150–51
Kart Championships 94
Katayama, Takazumi 105, 163
Kavanagh, Ken 17–18, 29, 187
Kawasaki 43, 94, 162
Keel, Jack 19
Keeler, Bob 28, 42, 46
Keevil 38, 48, 57, 68
Keith, Gordon 153
Kennedy, Frank 167
Kennell 121, 133
Kensington 11
Kerromoar 160
Keys, Basil 31, 36, 41
Kickham, E. 24
Kiddie, John 97, 127, 133
Kildress 172
Killalane 190
Killinchy 166, 173, 175
Killough 166, 175
Killyree 180
Kimnel Park 144
Kincardine 121
King, Alastair 42, 82, 88, 123–24, 126, 130, 187
Margaret King 10
Kingston-upon-Hull Festival 87
Kingston-upon-Hull Trophy 87
Kinmel Park 137, 143

Kinnaird, Tom 134–36
Kirkcaldy 122–24, 132, 135–36
Kirkcaldy Grand Prix 122
Kirkistown 166, 175–76
Kirkmichael 13, 156, 158, 160
Kitchen, Les 70
Kiyonari, Ryuichi 44
Knight, Ray 36
Knockhill 121, 129, 134–36
KTT Velocettes 122
Kuhn, Gus 19, 26
Lacey, Bill 24–25
Lancefield, Steve 18
Langbaurgh 85, 101
Lansivouri, Tepi 105
Lashmar, Denis 42, 47
Launchbury, Fred 36, 139
Lawton, Syd 41–42, 46
Layton, T.C. 102
LCC 33, 36, 85
Le Mans 15, 117
Leconfield 95
Lee Enfields 11
Leicester Query Club 60, 71
Leigh, George 110
Les Graham Trophy 114
Light Car Club 41, 84
Lisburn & District MCC 177
Lister, R. 129
Little Britax 147
Little Lurgan 177
Little Rissington 38, 48–51
Liverpool 59, 70, 108, 110, 112, 129
Llandow 137, 144–45
Llangollen 62
Loch Lomond Motor Cycling Club 133
Locke-King, Hugh 13
Lockett, Johnny 18, 25, 29, 36, 39, 41, 152
Lomas, Bill 10, 56, 62, 75, 87, 104, 187
London 14–15, 18–19, 26–28, 32–33, 35, 69, 128
Long Kesh Airfield 166, 177
Long Marston 14, 31, 58, 70–71

Longridge 108, 112
Lord March 30
Loughbrickland 168
Lougher, Ian 105
Louth 89, 190
Lurgan Park 166, 177
Lydden Hill 14, 19, 31–32
Lyons, Ernie 152, 169
McAllister, Alastair 130
McAlpine, Tony 17
McCallan, Phillip 188
McCandless, Cromie 152, 173, 179–80
McCandless, Rex 169
McConnachie, Ian 71
McCosh, Bill 175, 178
McCracken, Willie-John 180
McCulloch, Ray 155, 177
McCullough, Ray 178, 185
McElnea, Rob 105
McGarrity, Patsy 178
McGregor, Bob 124
McGregor, Ian 178
McIntyre, Bob 40, 82, 88, 105, 108, 115, 121–25, 129–30, 133, 136, 138, 152, 154, 157, 182, 187
McKindlay, Peter 95
McLaren, Bruce 30
McMinnies, W.G. 13
McNeilly, A. 179
Maghaberry 166, 168, 177–78
Maghaberry circuit 168, 178
Mallory Park 9, 21, 58, 60, 71–75, 116, 146, 149
Manchester 111–12
Manley, Mick 82, 147
Mann, Dick 116
Mann, Ronnie 133
Mansfield 79, 91–93
Manx Grand Prix 36, 128, 139, 150–53
Manx Norton 25, 28, 45, 88, 91, 107, 122, 143, 186
Marks, Rob 36
Marshall, Roger 95, 110, 116
Martin, Guy 105

Matchless 24, 57, 78, 96, 113, 117, 138, 156, 171, 182–83
Mates, Charlie 37
Matthews, R.T. 180
Mavrogordato, Noel 84
Mawdsley, Kevin 111
MCC 14, 27, 33, 36–37, 43, 45, 57, 60–61, 68, 70, 79, 135, 146, 154, 168, 173, 175–77
MCC & LCC 33, 36
MCRRC 168
Mead, Nigel 154
Mead, Ronnie 90, 179
Meagan, Harry 151
Meek, Chris 73
Meier, Georg 157
Melbourne 64–66
Mellor, Phil 95, 98, 104–05
Mellors, Ted 27, 65, 99
Melville Club 126–27, 129
Menai Straight 149
Merrill, Ralph 151
Mid-Antrim Motor Club 179
Middlesbrough 101, 106–07
Middleton, Peter 60
Miller, Sammy 175, 182
Mills, Steve 128
Milne, Bill 127
Minihan, Ed 15
Minshull, R.J. 63
Minter, Derek 15, 19–20, 28, 31, 40, 42, 82–83, 114–15, 158, 182
Mockford, F.E. 26
Mold 147
Moles, Thomas 185
Mona 137, 145
Mona Airfield 145
Monaghan – Glaslough circuit 166, 180
Monahan Circuit 190
Mondello Park 190
Monty, Geoff 35, 41, 46, 52, 55
Moodie, Jim 125
Moreton Valance 38, 50–51
Morpeth 107
Morris, Phil 10

Morrison, Brian 83
Mortimer, Charles Snr 25, 51, 163
Morton Valence 50
Moss, Stirling 30
Moto GP 66, 120
Moto Guzzi 18, 28, 34, 36, 47, 53–54, 59, 61, 72, 81, 113, 143, 157, 187
Motor Circuit Development Ltd 21, 115
The Motor Cycle 11, 15, 17, 22, 25–26, 32, 53, 59–60, 77, 80, 83–84, 89, 101, 109, 116, 136, 140, 151, 156, 178
Motor Cycle News (MCN) 19, 22, 48–49, 65, 83, 116–17, 126
Motor Cycle News Superbike Championship 22, 83
Motor Sport Vision 22, 116
Mottram, John 10
Moult, H.W. 72
Mountain Circuit 150–51, 153, 159, 164–65
Mountain Course 9, 156–57, 165
Mourne Motor Club 169
MOV Velocette 141
Muir, Dougie 127
Muir, Susan 10
Munks, Austin 84, 152
Murgatroyd, Jack 96
Murray, Steve 62, 78, 97, 117, 169
Museum of Flight 129
MV Agusta 17–18, 20, 28, 46, 54, 59, 78, 96, 108, 114, 158, 160
Mynydd Eppynt 140
Nadin, Brian 62
Nantwich 148
Nation, Trevor 43
Nelson, Billie 145
New Addington 15
Newbold, John 110, 116
Newcastle 102, 107, 124
Newcastle-upon-Tyne 102
Newman, G. 31
Newmarket 33, 36–37
Newtownards Airfield 176
Newtownards Airport 166, 180

Nicholson, Bill 169, 177
Nickels, Chris 57
Nicoll, D. 131
Nixon, Gary 116
Norris, F. 152
North Armagh MCC 177
North Down Club 180
North East London Cup 15
North East London MC 35
North East London MCC 14
North Gloucester Road Racing 44
North Gloucestershire MCC 43, 45, 57, 68
North Manchester Motor Club 111
North of Ireland Motor Club 182
North Wales 143, 145, 147
Northern Ireland 9, 11, 150, 166–67, 169, 171, 173–75, 177, 179, 181, 183, 185, 187, 189
Norton 17–18, 20, 25, 27–28, 31, 33–34, 39–43, 45–47, 50, 53–56, 59–62, 65, 70, 76, 78, 87–88, 97–98, 100, 102, 104, 109, 111, 113–15, 117–18, 124, 126, 129, 132, 142–43, 147, 151–52, 154, 157–58, 168, 171, 173, 175, 177–78, 180–81, 183, 186–87
Norton Dominator 129
Norton Rotary 43
Norvil Commando 56
Norwich 34–35
Notman, Leigh 36
Nottingham Tornados 59
NSU 34, 42, 76, 78, 96, 147, 159
O'Donovan, Daniel 24
O'Rourke, Michael 46
Oldham, Dennis 57
Oliver's Mount 103–04, 106
Oliver, Eric 36, 61, 90, 101, 104
Onchan 165
Orme, Rob 104
Ormesby Hall 85, 101
Ormskirk 112
Orr, Neol 183
Osmaston Manor 58–60, 75–76

Oswestry 62, 76
Oswestry Club 62
Oulton Park 9, 21–22, 35, 54, 73,
    93, 108, 113, 115–16, 123,
    133, 147
Ouston 85, 102
Paddington 14, 33
Paddington Recreation Grounds 33
Padgett, Don 97
Page, Greg 36
Palmer, Chris 105
Palmer, Jonathan 22, 35, 93, 116
Pantell, Gordon 139, 150
Park Hall 58, 62, 76–77
Parkinson, Denis 35, 68, 86, 88,
    100, 104, 111, 113, 123, 143,
    152
Parry, Len 138
Patrick, John 10, 72, 155
Patrickson, Steve 71
Payne, Ginger 15, 42, 45
Peetman, Alec 124
Pegasus MC 85
Pembrey 73, 137, 146
Pendennis Castle 38, 51
Pendlebury, Dave 52
Pentith Climb 119
Perris, Frank 47
Perth 130
Perton 58, 78
Petty, Ray 31, 41
Peugeot-Norton 156
Phillips, Tom 138, 148
Phillips, Wal 24
Phoenix Park 190
Piccadilly Circus 141
Pickering, Vee 99
Pickrell, Ray 28
Pidcock, Fred 10, 144–45
Pike, David 10
Pike, Roland 16–17, 29, 35, 39, 41
Pirie, Doug 151
Pladdys, Ron 51, 78, 145, 147
Plater, Steve 44
Plenderleith, Archie 10
Plenderlieth, George 131
Plymouth 38, 51

Plymouth Central Park 51
Plymouth Motor Club 51
Ponti, Ron 71
Poole, Tim 148, 149
Pope, Bob 106
Pope, Noel 25, 27, 39
Port Erin 153
Port St Mary 153
Portavogie 176
Portland Hairpin 68
Portrush 181
Portsmouth 57
Portstewart 181–82
Potter, Dave 28, 92
Powell, Keith 137
Powell, Martin 148
Pratt, Dennis 91, 102
Prees Heath 5, 58, 78
Preston 71, 106, 112, 119
Preston, M. 71
Provini, Tarquinio 160
Pryse, Marion 138
Purslow, Brian 59
Purslow, Fron 68, 76, 78, 147
Purvis, George 183
RAC 11, 80–81, 94, 98, 102
RAC British Car Sprint
    Championships 94
Race of the Year 73, 167–68
RAF Elvington 98
RAFMSA 36, 57
Raleigh 63, 170
Rallycross 31, 146, 149
Ramsey 13, 160–62
Randles, Len 151
RASC 39
Rathgormack 191
Rathkenny 179–80
Rayborn, Cal 22, 116
Read, Brian 188
Read, Phil 15, 28, 42, 45, 60,
    82–83, 92, 97, 105, 138, 152,
    154, 158, 187
Redfern, Ken 97
Redman, Jim 82, 187
Reeve, Peter 10
Reg Deardon Special 154

Reid, Dave 97
Rensen, Ralph 175, 183
Retford 58, 79
Revett, Geoff 34
Reynolds, John 43, 83
Rhodes, Ivan 63
Rhydymwyn 137, 147
Rhyl 143
Richards, Brian 97
Richmond 29
Ringwood Club 46
Robb, Tommy 82, 169, 171, 175, 185
Roberts, Elwyn 10
Roberts, Kenny 22, 75
Robertson, Bill 133
Robinson, Mervyn 167
Rochester 19
Rockingham Castle 9, 58, 79–80
Rodgers, R. 152
Rogers, Stu 98
Rollason, Nigel 51
Rolls, Charles 11
Romaine, Peter 81
Rosier, Jake de 24
Rous, Charlie 19, 31
Royal Enfield 76
Royal Highland Showground 133
Royce, Henry 11
Rudge 31, 41, 77, 151, 179, 185
Rudge, John 78
Rufford 68
Rufforth 85, 102
Rugby 62
Rusk, Walter 187–88
Russell, Gordon 36
Rutter, Michael 44
Rutter, Tony 78, 95, 110, 182
Ryder, Don 63
Rymer, Terry 83
Saarinen, Jarno 105
St Andrews 124
St Angelo 167, 183
St Athan 137, 147–48
St Dunstans 30
St Eval 38, 51–52
Salt, George 114

Sanby, Charlie 31, 56
Sandford, Cecil 17, 29, 52–53, 59, 62, 104, 138, 141–42, 187
Scarborough 9, 67, 85, 102–07
Schneidegger, Fritz 105
Scivyer, Brenda 10
Scivyer, Rod 49, 57
Scotland 9, 117, 121, 123–29, 131, 133–36
Scottish Classic Motorcycle Racing Club 129
Scottish Road Races 122–23
Sculthorpe 14, 33
Seahouses 86
Seamer Moor 103
Sear, John 97, 112
Sear, Oliver 33, 35
Selby, Howard 133
Senior Manx Grand Prix 128
Senior TT 114, 157, 160, 163, 168
Sennybridge 140
Serafini, Dorino 187–88
Setchell, Brian 42
Sevenoaks 15
Seward, Barry 36
Shaw, Jimmy 175
Sheene, Barry 22, 43, 67, 75, 83, 92, 98, 104–05, 115–16, 138
Sheffield 68, 107
Shepherd, Alan 96, 105, 152, 182
Shepherd, Terry 59–60, 129, 154
Sherry, Robin 16–17, 41, 53
Sherrygrim Circuit 172
Shields, A.P. 66
Shimmin, Danny 165, 173
Shipley 100
Shorey, Dan 15, 42, 45, 105, 109
Sidecar TT 156
Silloth 108, 117, 119
Silverstone 9, 16, 29, 53, 58, 66–67, 70, 80–84, 185
Simcock, Arthur 12
Simmonds, Dave 42, 97, 148
Simmonds, Mike 37
Simpson, Bill 127, 133
Simpson, Ian 125
Simpson, Jimmy 187

Skerries 191
Sleaford 85
Smart, Paul 28, 83, 182
Smith, Bill 16, 62, 78, 113, 154, 169, 171
Smith, Bob 105
Smith, Cyril 16, 36, 41, 53, 113
Smith, Tony 95
Snaefell Mountain 13
Snelling, Bill 10
Snetterton 9, 14, 21, 22, 33–35, 73, 93, 116
Snetterton Market 35
Solway Firth 117
Solway Motor Cycle Racing Club 117
Sousson, Vic 146
South Cheshire Motor Club 148
South Derry Club 173
South Downs 29
South Lethans 134–35
South Tees Motor Sport Park 106
South Wales Auto Club 145
Southampton 36, 53–54
Southampton & District MCC 36
Southern Circuit 150, 153, 165
Southern Ireland 190
Southern MCC 154
Southport 110, 112
Spann, Tommy 99
Speedway 26–27, 79, 111, 146
Spence, Ray 177
Spencer, Tony 34
Sportmax 34, 78, 159
Spray, Steve 43
Stainer, H.W. 11
Stanley, G.E. 24
Stapleford Tawney 14, 35–36
Staverton 38, 52
Steam Packet Company 156
Steele, Bob 127, 129
Steenson, Brian 169, 175, 178
Stenning, Canon E.H. 151
Stewart, James 175
Stewarts & Lloyds MCC 79
Stoke-on-Trent MCC 70
Stone, Nigel 95

Storr, John 17, 46
Stowe 81
Straight, F. 13
Stratford 70
Stratford-upon-Avon 84
Strawford, Howard 43, 44
Streatham 27
Sulby Bridge 160
Sunbeam 111, 151, 185
Supermoto 176
Surridge, Victor 24
Surtees, Jack 14, 27, 41, 53, 90
Surtees, John 16–17, 19–20, 28, 34, 40–42, 47, 54, 88, 105, 109, 138, 175, 187
Sutton Veney 38, 47, 52
Suzuki 37, 43, 48, 66–67, 92, 94, 115–16, 127, 134, 158, 165, 168–69, 182
Swain, Beryl 37
Swallow, Bill 173
Swansea 143
Swindon 57, 68
Sydare 174
Sydenham 26–27
Syston 58, 84
Syston Park 84
Tait, Percy 47, 55, 82, 105, 162
Tallaght 191
Tandragee 167, 177, 183
Tanner, Geoff 152, 171
Taylor, Arthur 141
Tayside Classic Motor Show 132
Teesside Autodrome 85, 106
Temple, C.F. 24–25
Tettenhall 78
Texaco Oil Company 129
Thorgold, Sir John G. 84
Thornaby 85, 107
Thornaby Airfield 107
Thorney Island 14, 36
Thorp, Tom 45
Three Sisters 108, 119–20
Thruxton 38, 40, 53–56, 73, 115, 146
Titanic British Championship races 115

Todd, George 41, 107
Tonfanau 137, 148
Topham, Mrs Muriel 108
Torrey Canyon 52
Tourist Trophy 11–12, 99, 150–51, 156, 165, 185
Transatlantic Challenge Series 22, 116
Transatlantic Trophy 22, 35, 75
Tranwell 85, 107
Tranwell Airfield 107
Tricoglus, Norman 128
Triumph 13, 19, 28, 39, 42, 47, 52, 55, 60, 62, 75–76, 87, 97, 113, 132, 141, 147–48, 152, 168–69, 178
Trollope, Dennis 36, 51
Trotter, Les 127
Trow, Alan 15, 20
Trowbridge 48
TT Mountain circuit 151, 153
Turnbury 121, 136
Turner, Ken 10
Tuttey, George 24
Twemlow, Ken 151
Ty Croes 137, 140, 149
Tyler, Arthur 84
Tynwald Hill 156
Tywyn 148
Ubbiali, Carlo 187
Ulster 63, 133, 167–69, 171–72, 174–75, 180–81, 183, 185–89
Ulster Grand Prix 63, 167, 174–75, 180, 183, 186–89
Ulster Motor Cycle Club 189
Undercliff Memorial Hall Fund 100
Uphill, Malcolm 49, 55, 139, 145
Upton, J. 27
Uttoxeter 58, 62
Vack, Herbert Le 24
Veloce 31
Velocette 17, 31, 33, 39, 47, 52, 70, 72, 77, 87, 89, 96, 101–02, 126, 131, 141–43, 151, 157, 173, 179–81
Villiers 132

Vincent 16–17, 19, 31, 34, 52–54, 62, 69, 76, 87, 102, 107, 138
Vincents 16, 70
Walderstown 190–91
Wales 9, 137–39, 141, 143–49
Walker, Ernie 88
Walker, Graham 122, 185–86
Walker, Murray 31, 104
Walker, Sir Ian 75
Wallasey 112
Wallis, Fred 59, 76
Walsh, P.J. 78
Ward, Hugh 10
Ward, Roy 118
Waterloo Club 110–11
Watton, Ivor 147
Watts, Nev 146
Webb, John 21
Weddell, Jock 130
Welfare, Pete 146
Wellesbourne 58, 84
Welsh, Rita 10
Welwyn Garden City 14, 37
West Park 85, 107
West Raynham 14, 37
West, Jock 25, 27, 65, 187
West, R. 96
Westhampnett 29
Westmorland, Mark 95
Weston-super-Mare 38, 56
Wetherby 102
Weybridge 13, 22
Wheatcroft, Tom 66
White City 9, 12
Whitham, James 43, 83, 105
Whitworth, David 25, 33
Wicklow 191
Wickstead, Ivor 25
Widdas, Jim 57
Wigan 116, 119
Wild, Pete 66
Wilkinson, Charles 89, 93, 101
Wilkinson, Jack 77
Wilkinson, Monty 89
Willaston 165
William Mark Holdings Ltd 31
Williams, Charlie 56, 105, 110, 155

Williams, Chris 63
Williams, H.L. 41, 143
Williams, John 22, 188
Williams, Peter 22, 28, 56, 105,
    182
Wilshire, Willie 63
Winfield 121, 124, 136
Wingfield Cup 76
Winter, Phillip 118
Winterburn, Roger 36
Wirral Hundred Motor Club
    112–13, 115, 143, 147, 149
Wolverhampton 78
Wood, Ginger 187
Wood, Tommy 14, 41, 47, 54, 77,
    89, 90, 101, 110
Woodcote 29, 81–83
Woodman, Derek 78
Woods, Stanley 27, 65, 157, 168,
    182, 187

Woods, Tommy 36
World Championships 185
World Superbike Championships
    22, 66, 116, 120
World War One 24, 64, 107, 144
World War Two 19, 22, 25, 27,
    30, 33, 51, 63, 71, 76, 97, 102,
    132, 150, 152, 157, 186, 189
Wormleighton, Clive 72
Wroughton 38, 57, 68
Wymering Park 38, 57
Yamaha 44, 57, 92, 94, 99, 105,
    111, 123, 146, 153, 155, 158,
    162, 167
York 98, 102, 107, 181
York Motor Club 107
Young, Derek 135, 180